Don't be overwhelmed with too much information in many All-In-One books. This laser-focus guide has been written in-depth and focused on Microsoft Word and Excel. This is to allow you to get valuable details from this book.

To all the learners, readers, beginners, and experts who embrace the power of technology, this book is for you. May it inspire confidence, spark creativity, and guide you toward mastering Microsoft Word and Excel with ease.

TABLE OF CONTENT

INTRODUCTION

Microsoft Office 365 is a cloud-based productivity suite that includes familiar applications such as **Word** and **Excel**. They are all designed to improve collaboration and streamline everyday tasks. Unlike traditional desktop versions of Office tools, Office 365 allows users to access these apps via the cloud. This means that you can work from virtually anywhere—on any device that connects to the internet.

Whether you're composing documents, creating spreadsheets, analyzing data, or organizing team projects, Office 365 provides all the tools you need to stay productive and organized, all integrated seamlessly into the cloud. Through **OneDrive**, another Microsoft software, your files are stored safely online, ensuring access across all your devices, and enabling collaboration in real-time.

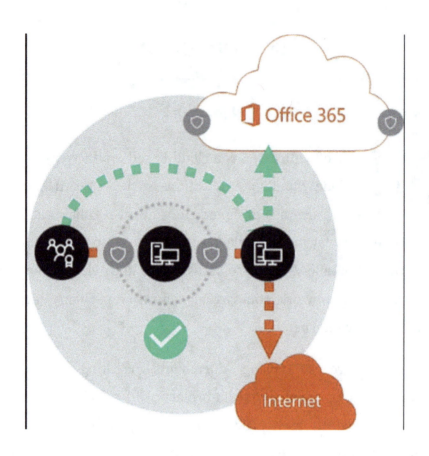

Benefits and Features of Cloud-Based App

Cloud-based applications like Microsoft Office 365 offer several key benefits:

- **Access From Anywhere, Anytime**: As long as you have an internet connection, you can access your files and work on them from any device (Windows, Mac, iOS, Android). This provides much needed flexibility for remote work or on-the-go productivity.

- **Collaboration in Real-Time**: Microsoft Office 365 is designed for easy collaboration. Whether you're working on a document in Word or building a spreadsheet in Excel, you and your colleagues can edit and comment on the same document at the same time.

- **Automatic Updates**: With Office 365, updates are automatically sent to your apps. You'll always have the latest features, security patches, and improvements, ensuring you are working with the most up-to-date tools.

- **Secure Cloud Storage**: With OneDrive, your files are securely stored in the cloud, accessible only to you or people you give access to. Automatic backups help safeguard your important documents, and file versioning allows you to restore previous versions if needed.

Saves Space   No maintenance cost   No technical knowledge   Enhanced Security

Multi Device Access   Scalable   Prevents Data Corruption   Easy Upload and Download

Advantages of Cloud Storage

Why Microsoft Office 365?

The key advantages of Office 365 are its **flexibility**, **integration**, and **collaboration** features.

- **Flexibility Advantage**: At home, in the office, or on the move, you can access your work documents from any device. This flexibility is essential for modern professionals who need to stay productive while balancing work and personal life.

- **Integration with Microsoft Tools**: Office 365 integrates well with other Microsoft tools. For example, your calendar in Outlook syncs with Teams, making scheduling meetings easier.

Documents created in Word can be shared directly through Teams for easy collaboration, and your Excel files can be uploaded and accessed from OneDrive.

How to Use This Book

This book is a guide with instructions for using each Microsoft Office 365 tool. The instructions are tailored for beginners, and relevant to experienced people too. It comes with easy-to-follow images and explanations. Each section will introduce a tool (Word and Excel,) and walk you through its basic functions, then progress to more advanced features.

As you go through the book, you'll get hands-on experience with real-world applications, ensuring that you not only understand the tools but can also apply them in your daily work tasks.

If you're new to Microsoft Office, don't worry—this guide is designed to help beginners, and you can take it in at your own pace.

This guide covers the following Microsoft Office 365 tools:

- **Microsoft Word**: Learn how to create, edit, and format documents, as well as collaborate on files with others.
- **Microsoft Excel**: Master spreadsheets, formulas, data analysis, and visualization techniques.

Each tool will have a dedicated section that covers its fundamental features and advanced capabilities. The below diagram shows many of the available Microsoft Office Applications. But in this book, we will be concentrating on just two of them: Microsoft Word and Excel

Chapter 1 – Getting Started with Microsoft Office 365

Before installing Office 365, it's essential to select the correct subscription plan. Microsoft offers several different options tailored to various types of users:

- **Personal Subscription**: This is ideal for individual users. This plan includes the full suite of Office apps (Word, Excel, PowerPoint, etc.) for one person, along with 1TB of OneDrive cloud storage. It's perfect for personal use and light work-related tasks.

- **Family Subscription**: This is a more affordable plan if you have multiple users at home. It allows up to 6 people to use Office 365, with each person getting their own 1TB of OneDrive storage.

- **Business Subscription**: This plan is designed for small businesses. It offers access to Office apps, 1TB of OneDrive storage per user, business email through Outlook, and advanced features for collaboration and security.

- **Student/Teacher Subscription**: If you are a student or teacher, you may qualify for Office 365 Education for free. This plan includes Word, Excel, PowerPoint, OneNote, and Microsoft Teams, along with OneDrive cloud storage.

Visit [Microsoft's subscription page](#) at https://www.microsoft.com/en-us/microsoft-365/get-started-with-office-365 to explore the available plans and choose the one that suits your needs.

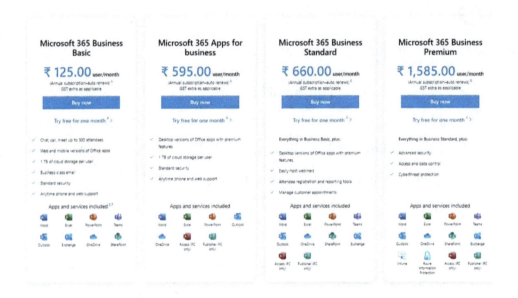

Installing Office 365 on Windows, Mac, and Mobile

After selecting your subscription, you can begin installing Office 365.

Below is a step-by-step guide for installing Office on various devices:

Installing Office on Windows:

Go to the [Microsoft Office download page](#) at: https://www.microsoft.com/en-us/microsoft-365/get-started-with-office-365

- Sign in with your Microsoft account. If you don't have one, create an account by clicking **Sign up**.
- Once signed in, click the **Install Office** button to download the installation file.
- Open the downloaded file and follow the on-screen instructions to complete the installation.

Once installed, launch any Office app (Word, Excel, etc.) and sign in with your Microsoft account to activate your subscription.

Installing Office on Mac:

- Visit the [Microsoft Office download page for Mac](#).
- Sign in with your Microsoft account.

- Download the Office installer for Mac.
- Open the installer and follow the prompts to install Office.

Once the installation is complete, open any Office app and sign in to activate it.

Installing Office on Mobile:

- For iPhone or iPad, go to the App Store and download Office apps like Word, Excel, and PowerPoint.
- For Android devices, visit the Google Play Store to download the Office apps.
- Once installed, sign in with your Microsoft account to start using Office on your mobile device.

Navigating the Office 365 Dashboard

When you first sign in to Office 365, you'll be taken to the homepage, where you can access all the Office apps and settings.

Office 365 Homepage:

This is where all your apps are. You will see large icons for the most commonly used apps such as **Word**, **Excel**, **PowerPoint**, and **Outlook**.

You can customize your homepage by pinning your favorite apps to the top for quicker access.

The **Search Bar** at the top allows you to search for documents, people, and apps across the entire suite.

Apps Menu:

The **App Launcher** (also called the "Waffle" icon) at the top-left corner opens the menu of available apps. Click this to explore additional apps like **Teams**, **OneDrive**, **Publisher**, and **Access**.

Click any app to open it in your browser or download it for desktop use.

Settings:

To access settings, click on your profile icon in the top-right corner and choose **Settings**.

From here, you can change your account settings, including notifications, themes, and language preferences.

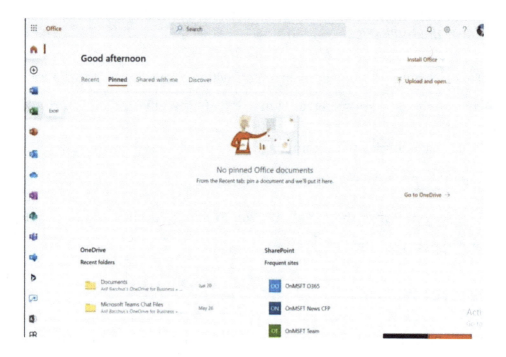

Creating and Managing Your Account

To fully enjoy the features of Office 365, you need a Microsoft account. If you don't already have one, here's how to create it:

- Visit the [Microsoft Account Signup Page](). At https://signup.live.com

- Enter your email address (or create a new Outlook or Hotmail email).

- Set a strong password and confirm it.

- Follow the prompts to verify your identity using a code sent to your email or phone.

- Once your account is set up, sign in to Office 365 with your new credentials.

You can also manage your Microsoft account settings by visiting the [Microsoft Account Management Page](). At https://account.microsoft.com/account

Personalizing Your Office 365 Profile

Once your account is set up, it's time to personalize your Office 365 experience:

- **Change Profile Picture**: Click on your profile icon in the top-right corner of Office 365. Select **Edit Profile**, and you can upload a photo of yourself to make your profile more personal.

- **Set Language Preferences**: If you prefer using Office in a different language, go to **Settings** > **Language and Region**, and choose your preferred language.

- **Security Settings**: Enable two-factor authentication (2FA) for added security. This ensures your account remains secure even if your password is compromised.

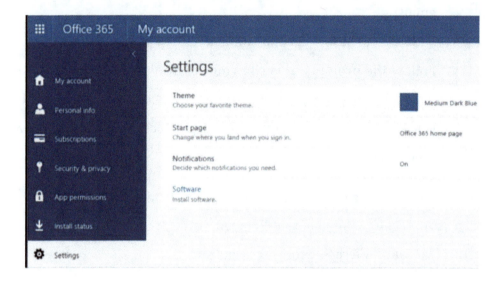

Chapter 2 – Microsoft Word for Beginners

Microsoft Word is one of the most widely used word processing programs, designed to help users create, edit, format, and share text-based documents. Whether you're writing a simple letter or a comprehensive report, Word offers a variety of tools to ensure your document is professional and polished.

Core Functions of Microsoft Word:

- **Document Creation**: Start a new document from scratch or use a template.
- **Text Editing**: Edit and modify the text with features like copy, paste, undo, and redo.
- **Text Formatting**: Change font styles, sizes, and colors, and apply bold, italic, or underline.
- **Page Layout**: Set margins, adjust line spacing, and choose the document's page size.
- **Collaboration**: Share documents with others and work on them simultaneously using Word's collaboration tools.

Word is designed to be intuitive and very accessible, whether you're a beginner or an experienced user.

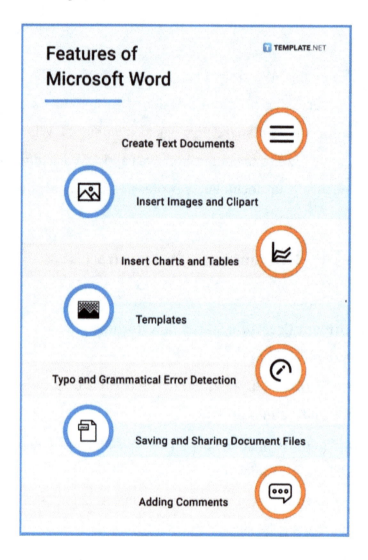

How to Create and Save Documents

Creating and saving a document in Word is a simple process:

Creating a New Document:

- Open Microsoft Word and click on **File** > **New**.
- You can create a blank document or select from various templates. To start a new document, click **Blank Document**.
- A new blank document will open, and you can start typing immediately.

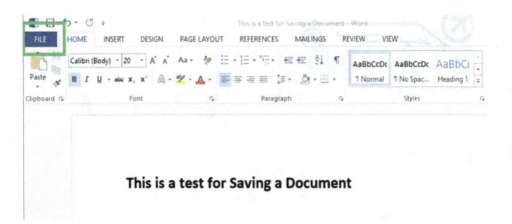

Saving Documents:

- To save your document, click on **File** > **Save As**.
- You'll be prompted to choose a location. Select either **OneDrive** for cloud storage or **This PC** to save it locally.
- Type a name for your document in the **File Name** field and click **Save**. The first time you save, you'll need to choose the folder where the document will be saved.

This is a test for Saving a Document

This is a test for Saving a Document - Word

Info

This is a test for Saving a Document
Desktop

Protect Document
Control what types of changes people can make to this document.

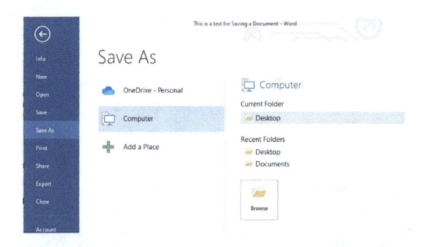

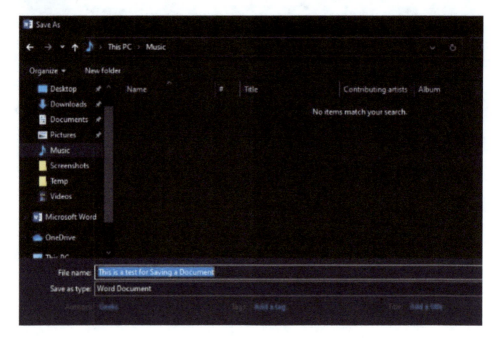

Saving Automatically:

If you saved your document in OneDrive, Word will save your document automatically as you work. You'll see the status at the top of the screen (e.g., "Saving..." or "Saved to OneDrive").

Navigating the Word Interface

Microsoft Word is organized around several key components:

Home Ribbon:

The **Home Ribbon** is the primary menu across the top of the Word window, containing commonly used tools such as font settings, paragraph alignment, styles, and clipboard functions (cut, copy, paste).

The ribbon is divided into sections such as **Font**, **Paragraph**, and **Styles**. Each section contains a set of related tools.

Quick Access Toolbar:

Located in the top-left corner, the **Quick Access Toolbar** allows you to add frequently used commands like **Save**, **Undo**, **Redo**, and **Print**.

To customize this toolbar, click on the small drop-down arrow next to it, and select the commands you want to add or remove.

Document Workspace:

The **Document Workspace** is the main area where you create and edit your document. It occupies the majority of the Word window and shows the content you're working on.

You can zoom in and out using the slider in the bottom-right corner or adjust the view by clicking on **View > Zoom.**

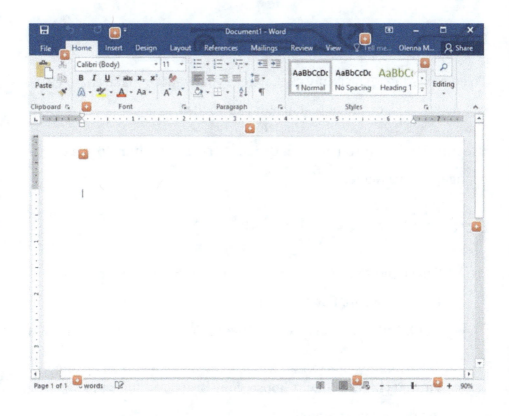

Basic Document Creation

Writing, Editing, and Formatting Text

Writing Text:

Simply click anywhere in the **Document Workspace** and start typing. Word will automatically adjust the text as you type, wrapping it to the next line when necessary.

Editing Text:

To edit existing text, simply click where you want to make changes. You can delete, add, or move text around as needed.

Use the **Undo** button in the **Quick Access Toolbar** to revert any changes you've made.

Formatting Text:

- Select the text you want to format and use the options in the **Home Ribbon**. For example:
- **Bold**, **Italic**, **Underline**: Use the respective buttons in the **Font** section.
- **Font Style and Size**: Choose your preferred font and size from the dropdown menus.
- **Text Color**: Click on the **Font Color** button to select a color.

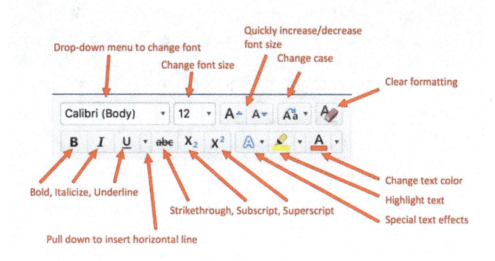

Drop-down menu to change font

Quickly increase/decrease font size

Change font size

Change case

Clear formatting

Bold, Italicize, Underline

Change text color

Highlight text

Special text effects

Strikethrough, Subscript, Superscript

Pull down to insert horizontal line

Displays the Font dialogue box.

Paragraph Formatting:

Adjust the alignment of text using the **Paragraph** section. You can choose **Left**, **Center**, **Right**, or **Justify** alignment.

Change line spacing by clicking **Line and Paragraph Spacing** in the **Paragraph** section and choosing your desired spacing.

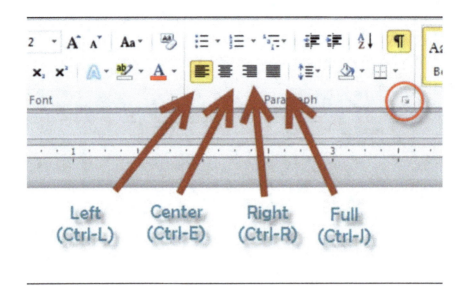

Left
(Ctrl-L) Center
(Ctrl-E) Right
(Ctrl-R) Full
(Ctrl-J)

Advanced Formatting and Tools

Inserting Images, Tables, and Other Media

Microsoft Word allows you to insert multimedia into your documents:

Inserting Images:

- Click on the **Insert** tab in the ribbon and select **Pictures**.
- Choose **This Device** to insert an image from your computer or **Online Pictures** to search the web for an image.

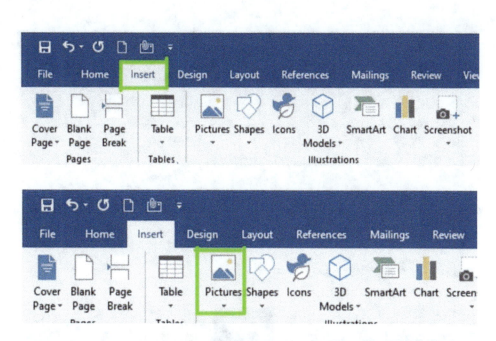

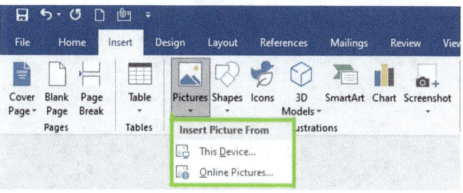

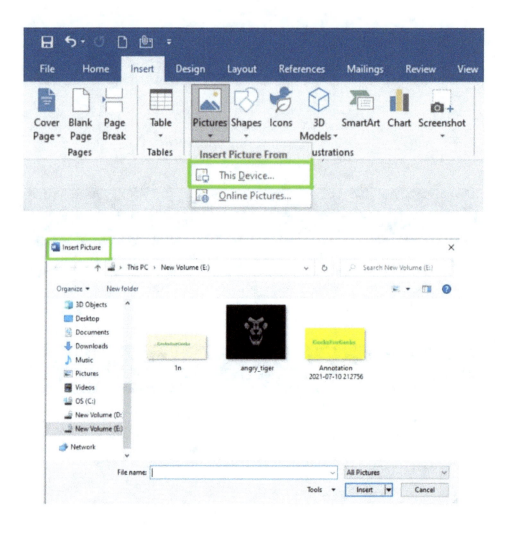

Inserting Tables:

Click on **Insert** > **Table**, then select the number of rows and columns you need.

You can adjust the table's layout, style, and colors using the **Table Design** and **Layout** tabs.

The table below shows a table of 3 columns by 4 rows. You drag your cursor across to choose the table you desire (number of rows and columns).

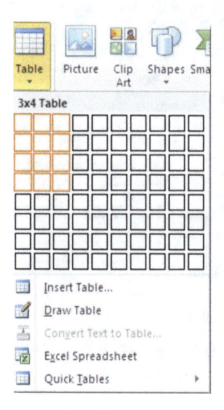

If the number of columns versus rows that you need more than the available one in the picture, select **Insert Table** below the boxes. For instance if the table you want to insert has 4 columns and 10 rows, the number of rows in the word template has only 8 rows, so you will need to select **Insert Table**.

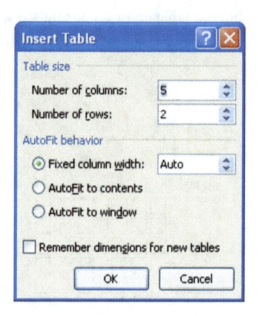

<u>*Adding Rows to a Table*</u>

- Select the Table:
- Click anywhere inside the table where you want to add rows. This will make the table visible with its gridlines and tools.
- Insert a Row Above or Below:
  - Hover your mouse over the row where you want the new one to appear.
  - Right-click on that row, and from the context menu, select **Insert**.

- Choose either **Insert Rows Above** or **Insert Rows Below**, depending on where you want the new row to go.
- Repeat for Multiple Rows:

To add several rows at once, highlight the same number of rows you want to insert, then use the **Insert** options. For example, selecting two rows and clicking **Insert Rows Below** will add two new rows.

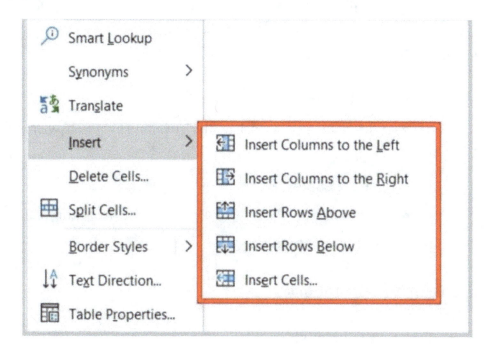

Adding Columns to a Table

- Select the Table Again:
- Click anywhere inside the table to activate it.
- Insert a Column Left or Right:

- Right-click on the column near where you want the new one.
- From the menu, select **Insert** and then choose **Insert Columns to the Left** or **Insert Columns to the Right**.
- Insert Multiple Columns:
  - Select several columns first and then insert more, just as you did for rows.

Deleting Rows from a Table

- Highlight the Row(s):
- Click and drag to select the row or rows you wish to remove.
- Use the Context Menu:
- Right-click on the selected row(s), and from the menu, choose **Delete Rows**.

Deleting Columns from a Table

- Select the Column(s):
- Hover over the column header area until your cursor changes to a downward arrow. Click to select the entire column.
- Remove the Column:
  - Right-click the selected column and select **Delete Columns** from the menu.

Inserting Other Media:

To insert other elements such as charts, shapes, or SmartArt, navigate to the **Insert** tab and choose from the options in the **Illustrations** section.

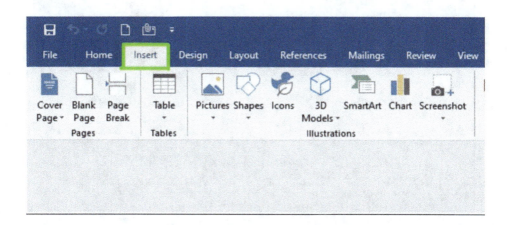

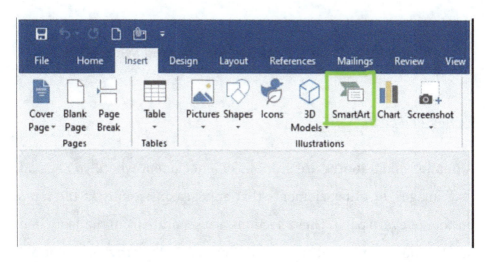

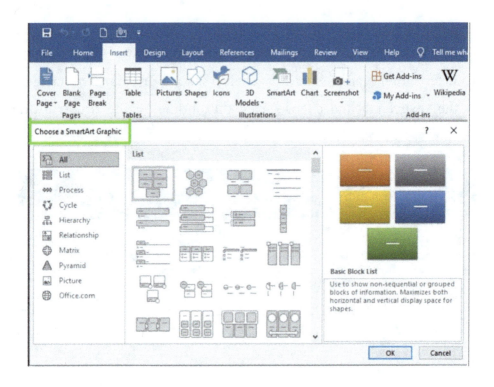

Using Header/Footer, Page Numbering, and Section Breaks

Header and Footer

A **header** and a **footer** are sections of a document where you can add text, images, or other elements that appear consistently at the top or bottom of every page. These sections are separate from the main body of the document and are typically used to provide additional information that remains constant throughout the document.

Header

The header is the area at the very top of each page. You can use it for:

- Document titles or chapter names
- Company logos or branding
- Author names or contact information
- Page numbers (if preferred at the top)

Footer

The footer is located at the bottom of each page. Common uses include:

- Page numbers (if not in the header)
- Dates
- Confidentiality notices (e.g., "Confidential" or "Draft")
- Document footnotes or references

How to insert Header and Footer

- Go to the **Insert** tab located at the top of the screen.

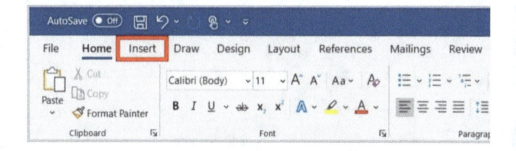

- In the toolbar, locate the **Header & Footer** group.

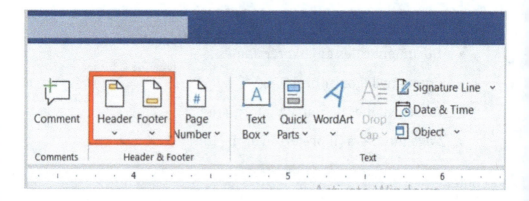

- Click on either **Header** or **Footer** depending on where you want your content to appear.
- A dropdown menu will appear showcasing various pre-designed templates for headers or footers.
- Pick one that suits the tone and purpose of your document.

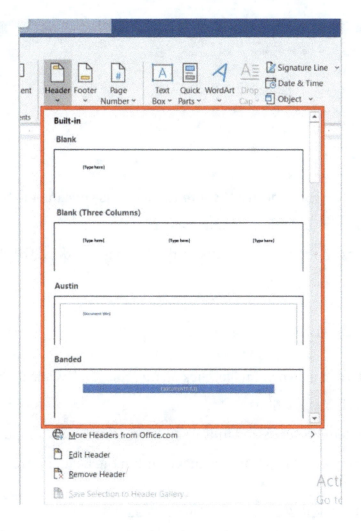

- If you want to start fresh, select **Edit Header** or **Edit Footer** at the bottom of the list.
- Once selected, the header or footer section will become editable.

- Type your desired content, such as document title, page numbers, Author's name, date, etc.
- Use the formatting tools in the toolbar to adjust the font style, size, and color.

Inserting Images or Logos to the Header or Footer

- To add a logo or image, click on the **Insert** tab while in the header or footer section.
- Select **Pictures** and upload an image from your computer.
- Resize and position the image within the header or footer area.

Adjust Margins and Layout of Header and Footer

- Click the header or footer area and go to the **Design** tab.
- Use the **Header from Top** or **Footer from Bottom** options to adjust the spacing.
- Align the content (left, center, or right) using the alignment tools.

Using Different Content for Odd and Even Pages

- If you need unique headers or footers on odd and even pages, tick the **Different Odd & Even Pages** option in the **Design** tab.

- Edit each header or footer separately to meet your requirements.

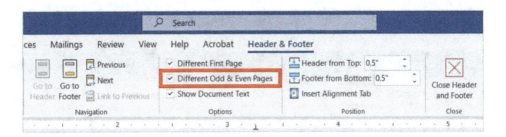

Removing Header or Footer from First Page

In the **Design** tab, check the **Different First Page** box.

Customize or leave the first-page header/footer blank while keeping the rest consistent.

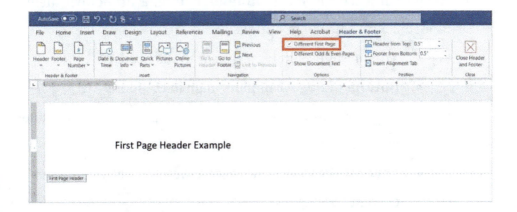

Page Numbering

Adding page numbers is a professional touch that helps readers navigate your work. Follow the following easy steps:

- At the top of your screen, locate and click on the **Insert** tab. This opens a menu filled with tools to enhance your document.

- Within the **Insert** tab, look for the **Page Number** button. It's typically in the **Header & Footer** section. Clicking this will reveal several options for placing page numbers.
- When you click the **Page Number** button, a dropdown menu appears with placement options like:
  - **Top of Page**: Numbers appear in the header.
  - **Bottom of Page**: Numbers align in the footer.
  - **Page Margins**: Numbers are displayed in the side margins.
  - **Current Position**: Inserts a number at the cursor's current spot.

- Select the placement style that best suits your document's layout.

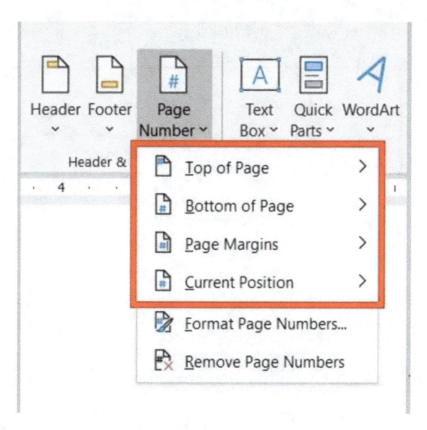

Once you've chosen the location, Word will display several formatting styles for the numbers. Scroll through and click on the one you prefer. You'll see a preview as you hover over each option.

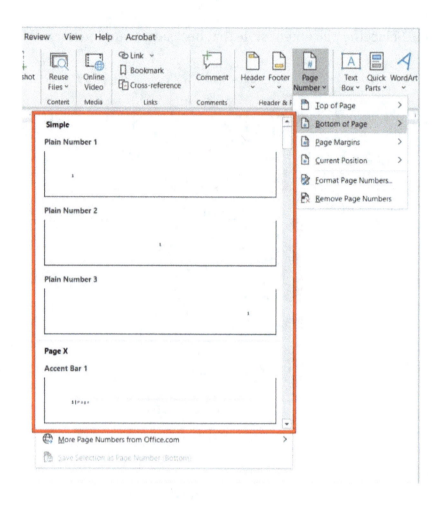

Adjusting the Format of Page Numbering

- If you'd like to customize how the numbers look (e.g., Roman numerals or letters), click **Format Page Numbers** in the dropdown menu. This allows you to tweak:
  - Number format (1, 2, 3 or i, ii, iii).

- Start at a specific number (ideal for sections starting mid-document).
- Click **OK** when you've made your adjustments.

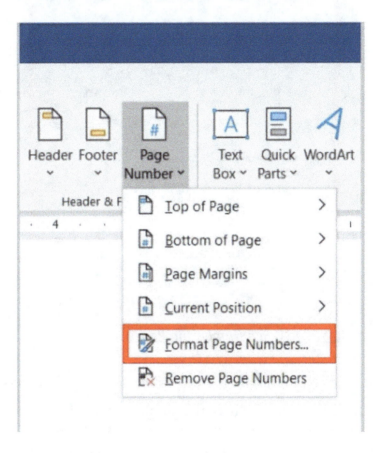

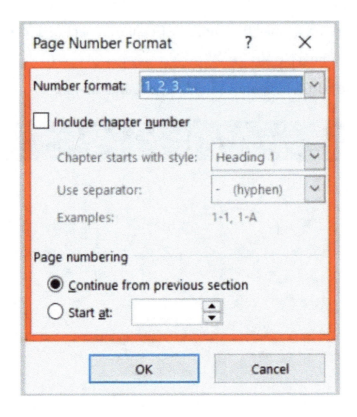

Excluding First Page When Numbering Pages

To leave the first page unnumbered—common for title pages—double-click the header or footer where the number appears. Then:

- Check **Different First Page** in the Header & Footer toolbar.

The first page will no longer display a number, while the rest of your document retains numbering.

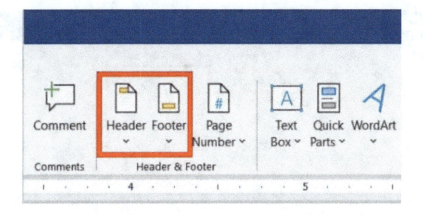

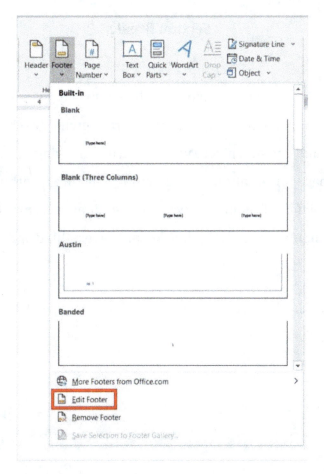

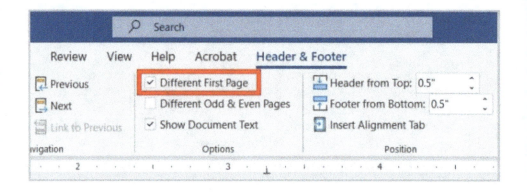

Section Breaks

Section breaks in Microsoft Word are like invisible dividers that let you split your document into distinct parts, giving each section its formatting and layout. They're very useful for changing headers, footers, margins, page orientations, or column structures within the same document. Think of them as a way to give different "chapters" of your document their unique style while keeping everything organized in one file.

- Go to the **"Layout"** tab on the ribbon (or "Page Layout" in older Word versions).

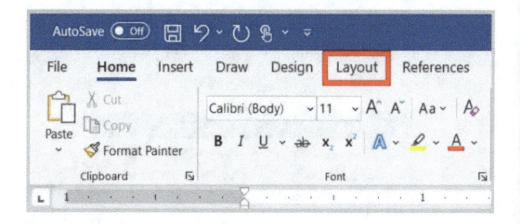

- Look for the **"Breaks"** option in the "Page Setup" group and click it.

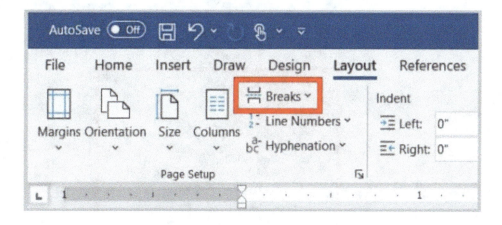

- Word offers four section break options. Pick the one that suits your needs: **Next Page**: Starts the new section on the next page. Perfect for chapter breaks. **Continuous**: Keeps the new section on the same page, ideal for changing formatting like switching to columns. **Even Page**: Begins the section on the next even-numbered page, useful for creating book layouts. **Odd Page**: Similar to "Even Page" but starts on the next odd-numbered page.

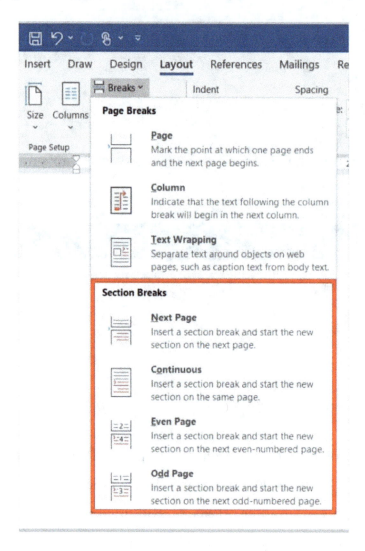

- After inserting the section break, adjust the formatting settings you want to customize for that section. For example: Modify headers or footers by double-clicking the area and editing them, Change page orientation to landscape or portrait via the **"Layout"** tab, and Switch the column layout under the **"Columns"** menu. Etc.

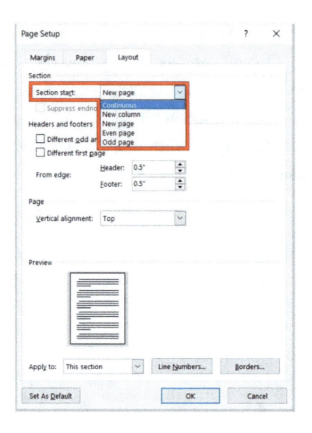

- If you want to see where your section breaks are located, go to the **"Home"** tab and click **"Show/Hide ¶"** in the "Paragraph" group. Section breaks will appear as dotted lines labeled with their type.

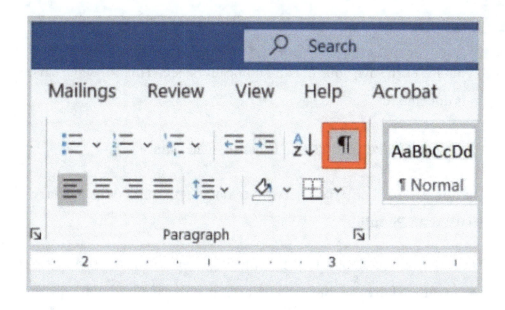

- To remove a section break, enable "Show/Hide ¶," click on the dotted line for the break, and press **Delete**.
- To edit a section, position your cursor in that section and apply new formatting changes.

Saving, Sharing, and Collaborating

Saving Documents to OneDrive:

Click **File** > **Save As** and select **OneDrive** as your storage location.

Your document will automatically sync with your OneDrive account, ensuring you can access it from any device.

Saving Locally:

If you prefer to save your document locally, select **This PC** when saving your document.

Sharing and Collaborating with Others in Real-Time

Sharing a Document: To share your document, click **File** > **Share** > **Share with People**.

You can invite collaborators by entering their email addresses or by copying the shareable link. We will discuss sharing in detail when we get to the chapter on Microsoft OneDrive.

Collaborating in Real-Time: Once your document is shared, multiple users can edit it simultaneously. Changes are automatically synced, and you can see who is working on the document in real-time.

Proofing and Reviewing Tools

Spell Check, Grammar Suggestions, and Thesaurus

Spell Check:

Microsoft Word automatically checks spelling as you type. Misspelled words are underlined in red.

Right-click on a misspelled word to see suggested corrections.

Grammar Suggestions:

Word also checks for grammar issues, which are underlined in blue.

You can review grammar suggestions by right-clicking on the underlined text.

Thesaurus:

Right-click on any word and select **Synonyms** to access the thesaurus and find alternative words.

Tracking Changes and Comments for Collaboration

Track Changes:

To track changes, click **Review > Track Changes**. All edits will be highlighted in the document.

You can accept or reject changes by right-clicking on them.

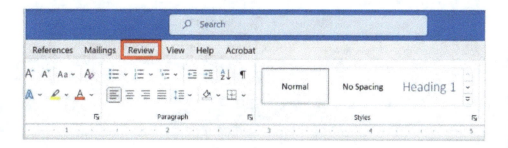

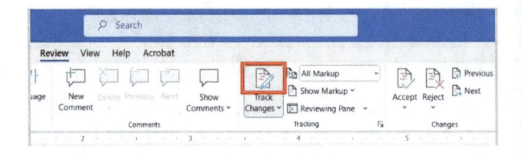

Adding Comments:

To add a comment, highlight the text you want to comment on and click **New Comment** in the **Review** tab.

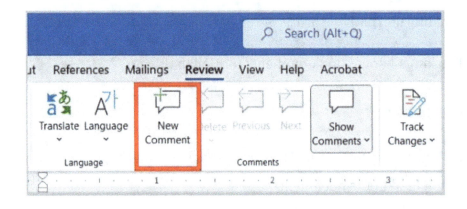

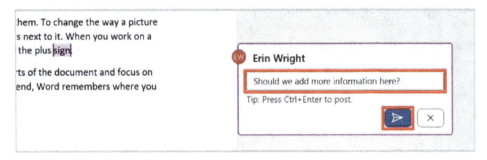

Chapter 3 – Microsoft Excel for Beginners

Microsoft Excel is a powerful spreadsheet program that allows you to create, organize, and analyze data. Whether you're tracking financial information, performing statistical analysis, or managing a project, Excel provides all the tools you need to organize your data efficiently and make informed decisions.

Key Uses of Excel:

- **Data Entry:** You can enter and store large amounts of data in Excel, including numbers, text, and dates.
- **Data Analysis:** Excel includes features such as sorting, filtering, and complex calculations for analyzing large datasets.
- **Visualization:** You can turn raw data into visual charts and graphs, making it easier to understand and present.
- **Automation:** By using functions and formulas, you can automate repetitive tasks and calculations.

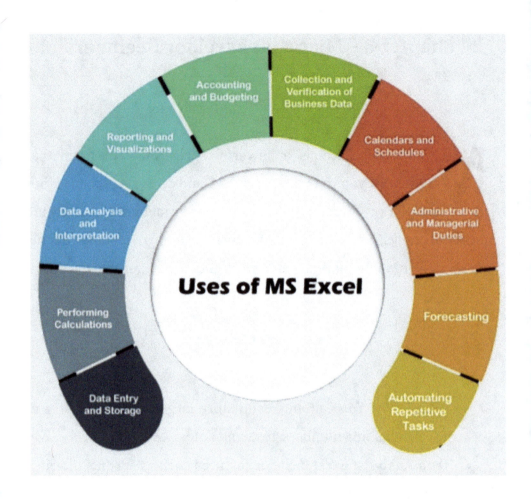

Opening, Saving, and Organizing Workbooks

- Opening Excel: To start Excel, click on the **Excel** icon in your Office 365 dashboard or your desktop. You can choose to create a new workbook or open an existing one.
- Creating a New Workbook: Once Excel is open, click on **New** and select a blank workbook or choose from templates available for different tasks (e.g., budget templates, inventory sheets, etc.).

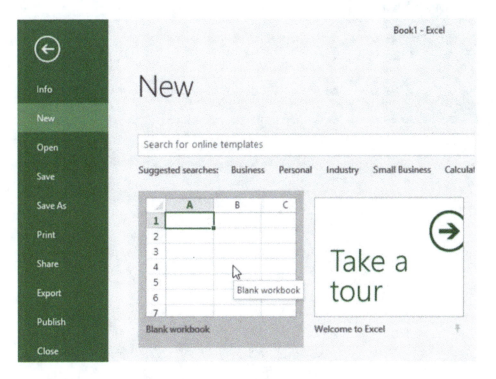

- To open a recent workbook, instead of selecting New, click **Open**.

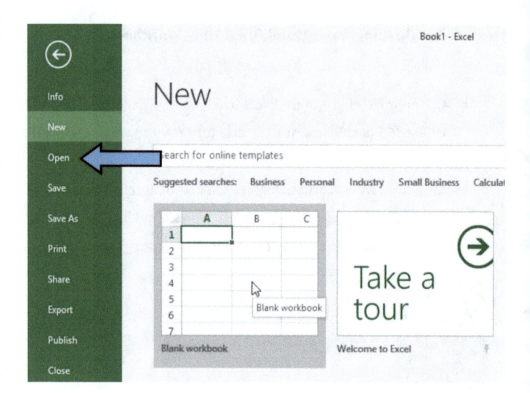

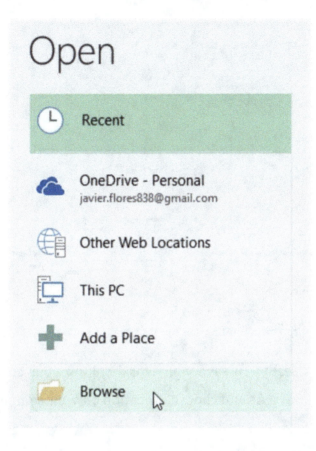

- A dialog box will open, locate t=and select the desired workbook, then click **Open**.

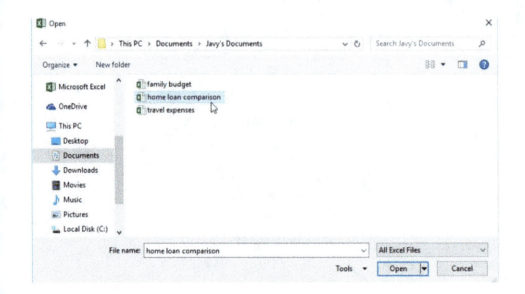

Saving a Workbook:

- Save Locally: To save your workbook on your computer, click
  File > **Save As** and choose a location on your computer.

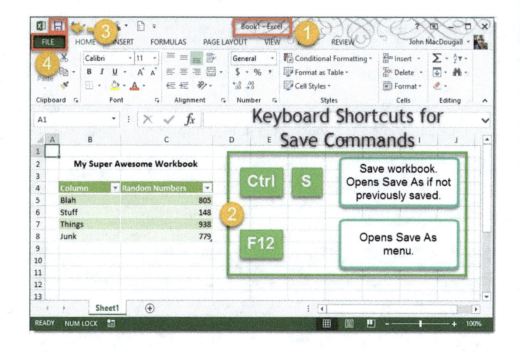

- Save to OneDrive: For cloud storage, choose **Save As** > **OneDrive** to ensure your workbook is accessible from anywhere and can be easily shared.

Organizing Workbooks:

Excel workbooks can consist of multiple worksheets, making it easy to organize your data. Each worksheet can represent a different dataset or aspect of a project. You can add, rename, or delete sheets by right-clicking on the sheet tab at the bottom of the screen.

Rename Your Worksheets

- Default names like "Sheet1," "Sheet2," and so on can quickly become confusing.
- Double-click the worksheet tab at the bottom of your Excel screen.
- Type a new, descriptive name, such as "Sales Data," "Employee List," or "August 2024" and press Enter.

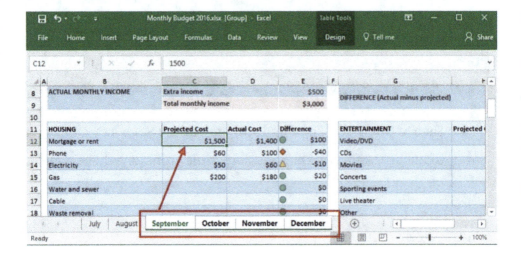

Rearrange Worksheet Tabs

Got your sheets in a jumble? Here's how to reorder them:

- Click and hold the tab of the worksheet you want to move.
- Drag it left or right until it's in the desired position.
- Release the mouse button, and voilà—it's reorganized!

64

Create a Table of Contents Sheet

If your workbook has many tabs, create a summary sheet for quick navigation:

- Insert a new worksheet at the beginning of your workbook.
- Name it "Table of Contents."
- List all your sheet names and hyperlink them by pressing Ctrl+K (Command+K on Mac).
- This acts like an index, instantly letting you jump to the desired sheet.

Navigating the Excel Interface

The Excel Ribbon, Formula Bar, and Cells

The Excel Ribbon:

The **Ribbon** at the top of the Excel window is where you'll find all the tools you need to work with your workbook. It's divided into tabs, such as **Home**, **Insert**, **Formulas**, and **Data**, each offering different options for managing your workbook.

For example, under the **Home** tab, you can find options to format text, change cell alignment, and apply styles.

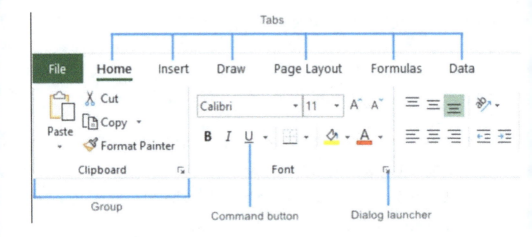

Formula Bar:

The **Formula Bar** is located directly above the worksheet and displays the contents of the selected cell. You can use the Formula Bar to edit data or enter formulas.

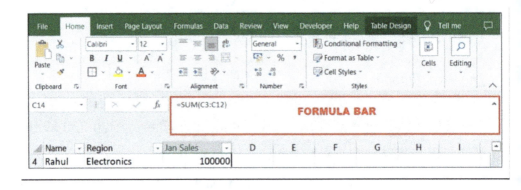

Cells:

Excel organizes data in a grid of cells, each identified by its **row** number (1, 2, 3, etc.) and **column** letter (A, B, C, etc.). Each cell can contain text, numbers, or formulas.

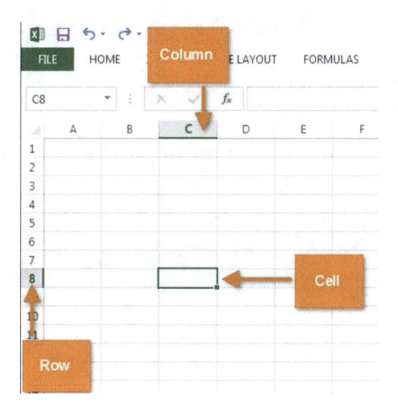

Worksheet vs. Workbook: Understanding the Structure

Workbook: A workbook is the entire Excel file, which can contain multiple worksheets (tabs).

Worksheet: A worksheet is a single tab within the workbook, where your data is entered. By default, a new workbook starts with three worksheets, but you can add more by clicking the **+** symbol at the bottom.

Each worksheet can represent a different set of data, making it easy to organize different categories or time periods.

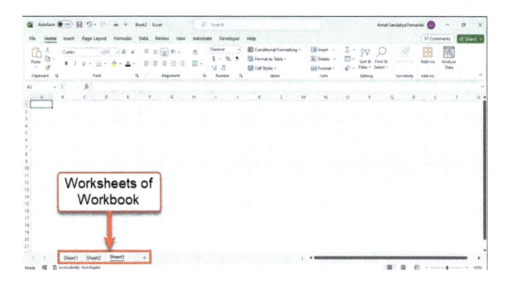

Basic Data Entry and Formatting

Entering Text, Numbers, and Dates

- **Text**: To enter text, click on the desired cell and begin typing. You can enter names, descriptions, or any other form of text.

- **Numbers**: To enter numbers, select a cell and start typing. Excel automatically recognizes numeric entries and aligns them to the right.

- **Dates**: To enter dates, simply type the date in a recognizable format (e.g., "MM/DD/YYYY"). Excel will automatically format the date in the default style for your region.

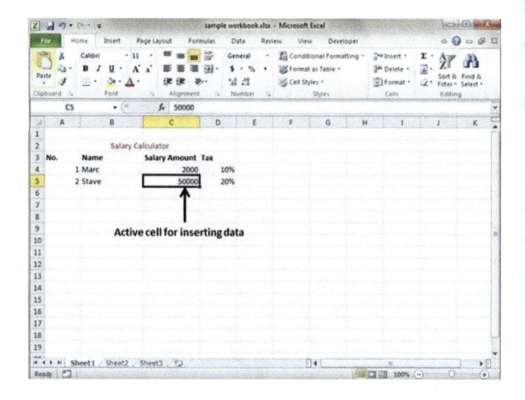

Formatting Cells (Text, Number, Currency, etc.)

- **Text Formatting**: To change the font, size, or color of your text, use the **Home Ribbon** options under **Font**.

- **Number Formatting**: To format numbers (e.g., for currency, percentages, or decimals), click on the cell, then select your preferred format under the **Number** section in the **Home Ribbon**.

- **Currency**: Use the Currency format to add dollar signs or other symbols for financial data.

Now, below is a step-by-step guide on how to format cells in your Excel worksheet:

Select the Cells You Want to Format

- Click and drag your mouse to highlight the cells that need some sprucing up. You can choose a single cell, a group of cells, or even an entire column or row.

Access the Format Cells Menu

- Right-click on the selected cells and choose **"Format Cells"** from the dropdown menu. Alternatively, press Ctrl + 1 (Windows) or Cmd + 1 (Mac) as a shortcut. A box with plenty of options will pop up, ready to transform your data.

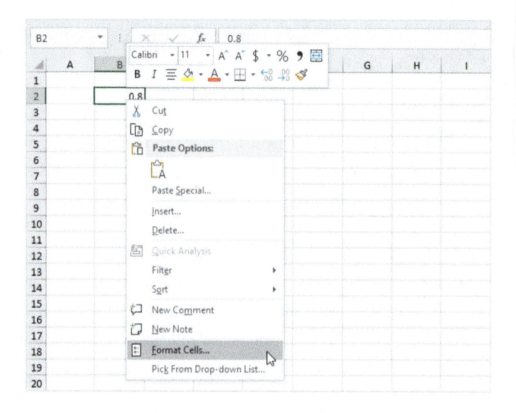

Choose a Category for Formatting

In the **Format Cells** dialog box, you'll see a list of categories on the left:

- **Text:** Choose this when your data consists of words, like names or descriptions. Excel won't try to interpret the content—it will leave it exactly as you type it.

- **Number:** Use this option to format numeric data. You can add decimal places or commas to make large numbers easier to read.

- **Currency:** Perfect for financial data. Choose a currency symbol (like $, €, or ¥) and decide how many decimal places you want to show.

- **Date:** Convert raw date entries into polished formats, like "MM/DD/YYYY" or "Month Day, Year." Excel will do the heavy lifting for you.

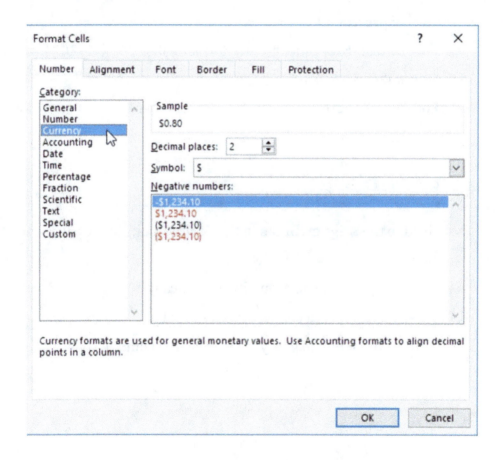

Customize Formatting Options

Once you've chosen a category, customize it to fit your needs:

- **For Numbers:** Decide on the number of decimal places and whether to add a separator (for example, "1,000").
- **For Currency:** Pick your preferred currency symbol and the level of precision.
- **For Dates:** Experiment with formats like "12/31/2024" or "December 31, 2024."
- **For Text:** There's not much to tweak here—Excel keeps it simple.

Align Your Data Perfectly

- Head to the **Alignment** tab in the **Format Cells** menu. Here, you can:
  - Center data horizontally or vertically.
  - Wrap text so it stays within the cell.
  - Rotate text to give your worksheet a unique style.

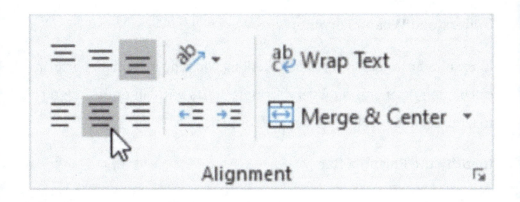

Working with Formulas and Functions

Basic Excel Formulas: SUM, AVERAGE, COUNT

- **SUM**: To calculate the sum of a range of numbers, type =SUM(A1:A10) into the cell, where A1:A10 is the range of cells you want to sum.
- **AVERAGE**: To calculate the average of a range, type =AVERAGE(A1:A10).
- **COUNT**: To count the number of cells with numbers in a range, use =COUNT(A1:A10).

These formulas will automatically calculate the sum, average, or count based on the data in the specified range.

Now, below is a step-by-step guide on how to work with formulas in your Excel worksheet:

Understand What a Formula Is

In Excel, a formula is a set of instructions you type in a cell to perform a calculation or operation. Every formula starts with an **equals sign (=)** to let Excel know you're doing math or logic.

Identify the Formula Bar

The **Formula Bar** is located at the top of the spreadsheet, just above the grid of cells. It's where you'll see or type your formulas. Click on any cell, and what you type in the cell will appear in the formula bar.

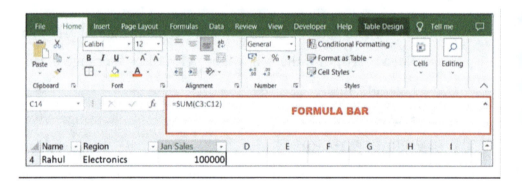

Simple Addition

Let's say you want to add two numbers:

- Click on a blank cell where you want the result to appear.
- Type =2+3 and press **Enter**.
- The cell will display the result, **5**.

This is how Excel processes basic addition.

Use Cell References

Instead of typing numbers directly, you can use cell references. This means pointing to other cells in your formula. For example:

- Enter **2** in cell **A1** and **3** in cell **A2**.
- Click on a blank cell, say **A3**, and type =A1+A2, then press **Enter**. Alternatively, you can click on the blank cell you choose, type = then click on the cells containing the numbers you want to add. Excel will add the numbers in the cells and show the result in the cell you chose.

Subtraction, Multiplication, and Division

You can use the same steps for other basic math operations:

- **Subtraction:** Use - (minus). For example, =10-4 or =A1-A2.
- **Multiplication:** Use * (asterisk). For example, =2*3 or =A1*A2.
- **Division:** Use / (slash). For example, =6/2 or =A1/A2.

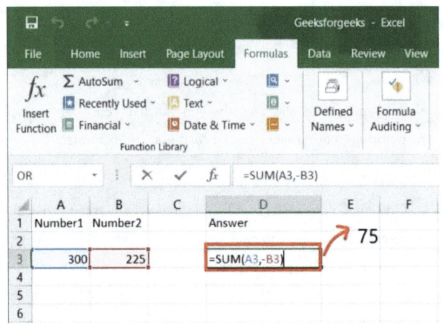

Excel SUBTRACTION Formula

SUM Function

The SUM function is a quick way to add up multiple numbers or cells.

- Type some numbers in cells **A1, A2, A3, and A4**.
- Click on a blank cell, and type =SUM(A1:A4), then press **Enter**.

Excel will add all the numbers from **A1** to **A4** and display the result.

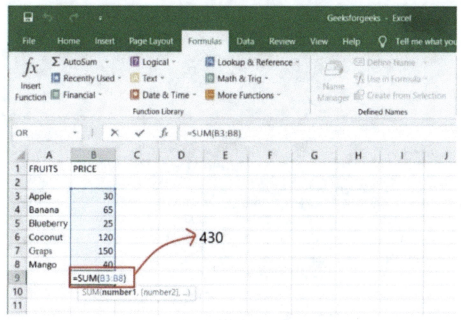

Excel SUM Formula

Alternatively, use the **AutoSum** button on the toolbar:

- Select the numbers in a column that you want to add

- Click on a blank cell where you want the total to appear

- Go to the **Home** tab, find the **AutoSum** button, and click it. Excel will guess the range and calculate the sum.

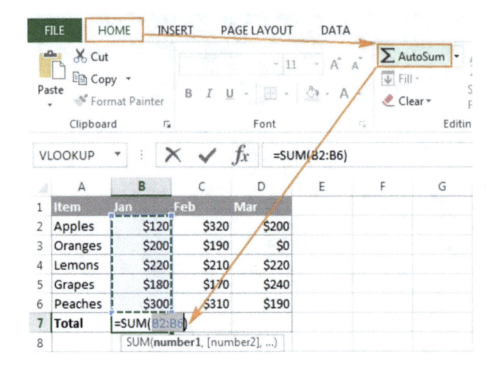

The AVERAGE Function

The AVERAGE function calculates the mean of a group of numbers.

- Enter some numbers in cells **B1, B2, and B3**.
- In a blank cell, type =AVERAGE(B1:B3) and press **Enter**.

Excel will calculate the average of those numbers.

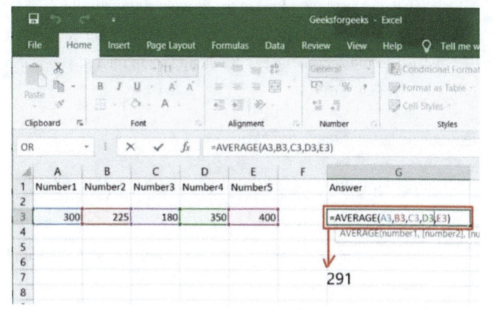

Excel AVERAGE Function

Using the AVERAGE Function

- Go to the **Formulas** tab in the toolbar at the top.
- In the **Function Library** group, click **More Functions**, then **Statistical**, and select **AVERAGE**.

Alternatively, you can use the **AutoSum dropdown** (found in the Home or Formulas tab) and select **Average**.

- A small box will appear asking for the range of cells to average.
- Use your mouse to select the range of cells containing the numbers (e.g., **A1:A5**).

- You'll see the range added to the formula automatically.

- Click **OK**, and Excel will calculate the average of the numbers in the selected range. The result will appear in the cell you chose earlier (e.g., **A6**).

Use AutoFill for Repeating Formulas

If you have a formula in one cell and need it applied to other cells:

- Click on the cell with the formula.

- Hover your mouse over the bottom-right corner of the cell until you see a small cross (+).

- Drag it down or across to copy the formula into other cells.

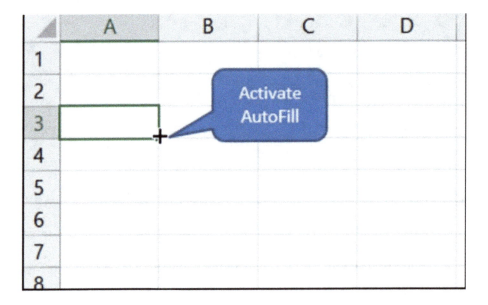

Understanding Cell References and Relative/Absolute References

Relative Reference: When you copy a formula from one cell to another, Excel automatically adjusts the references. For example, copying the formula =A1+B1 from one cell to another will change the references based on the new cell position.

Absolute Reference: To keep a cell reference constant, use the dollar sign ($). For example, =$A$1+$B$1 will always refer to cells A1 and B1, no matter where you copy the formula.

Advanced Excel Features

Conditional Formatting for Visual Cues

Conditional Formatting is a powerful tool in Excel that allows you to highlight cells with colors, icons, or data bars based on specific conditions. It's like telling Excel to make certain data stand out for easier analysis. Here's a simple step-by-step guide:

- Click and drag your mouse over the range of cells where you want to apply Conditional Formatting. This could be a single column, multiple columns, or even the entire sheet.
- Navigate to the **Home** tab in the ribbon at the top of Excel.

- Look for the **Styles** group, and click on **Conditional Formatting**.

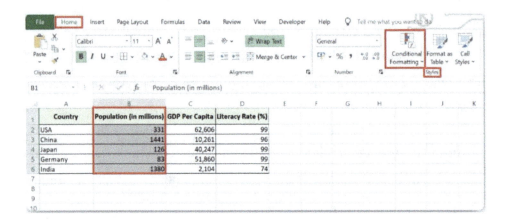

- Choose a Formatting Rule. You'll see several options. Choose the one that fits your needs:

  - **Highlight Cells Rules**: Use this to highlight values greater than, less than, or equal to a specific number, or to find duplicates.

  - **Top/Bottom Rules**: Highlight the top 10 items, bottom 10 items, or data above/below the average.

  - **Data Bars**: Add visual bars within cells to compare values.

  - **Color Scales**: Apply gradient colors to show the range of values.

  - **Icon Sets**: Add icons (arrows, traffic lights, etc.) for easy visual cues.

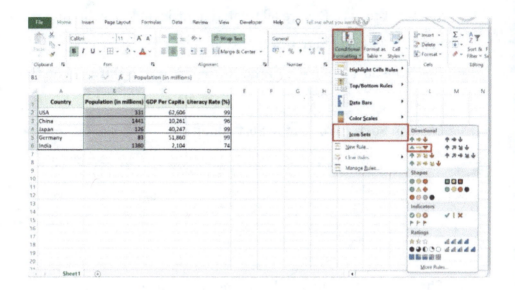

Once you select a rule, a dialog box will appear. Here's what you'll do:

- Define the condition. For example, if you choose **Greater Than**, enter the value, such as "50."

- Select the formatting style (e.g., a red fill, bold text, or a custom format).

- Preview how the formatting will look.

Sorting and Filtering Data

Sorting Data in Excel

Sorting helps you organize your data alphabetically, numerically, or by custom order. Follow these steps:

- Select the Data You Want to Sort. Highlight the range of cells you want to sort. Ensure all related data, including column headers, is selected to avoid mismatched rows.

- Open the Sort Menu. Go to the **Home** tab or the **Data** tab on the ribbon.

- Click on **Sort...** to open the Sort dialog box.

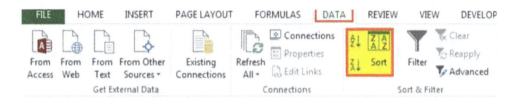

- Choose a Column to Sort By. In the sort dialog box, select the column you'd like to sort. For instance, if you're sorting a list of names, pick the "Name" column. If your columns are not named, it will be column A, B, C, etc.

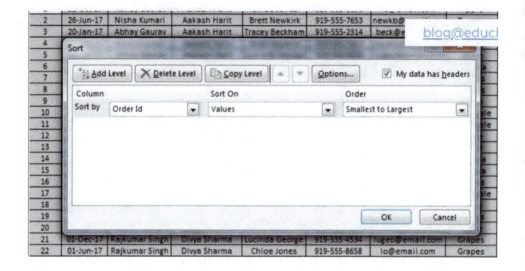

- Pick a Sorting Order. For text, choose between **A to Z** (ascending) or **Z to A** (descending).

- For numbers, choose **Smallest to Largest** or **Largest to Smallest**.

- Add Multiple Sorting Levels (Optional). If you want to sort by more than one column, click **Add Level**. For example, you can sort first by "Department" and then by "Name." In the image below, the sorting criteria given is to sort first by the name of the reporting manager, then the name of the employee, and then the total number of orders. All these are data represented by different columns that are being sorted.

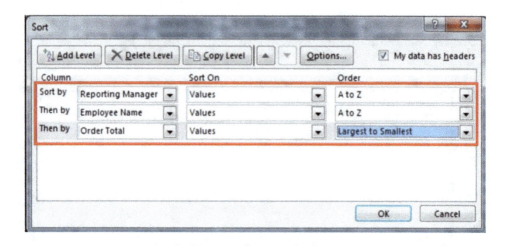

- Apply and Verify. Click **OK** to apply the sorting. Your data should now be arranged in the chosen order. Double-check to ensure the sort worked as expected. The result will look something like this below:

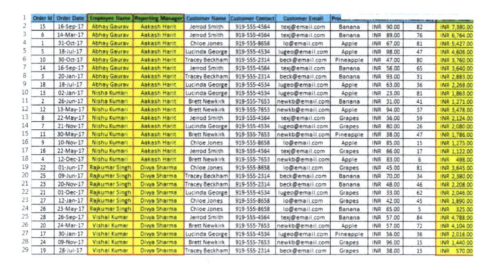

Practical Application of Sorting Data in Excel

Sorting data in Microsoft Excel has a wide range of practical applications, making it an essential tool for organizing and analyzing information. Here are some common applications of sorting data:

1. Organizing Large Datasets

When working with extensive lists, such as customer names, product inventories, or sales records, sorting helps bring order to the chaos.

Example: Arrange a customer list alphabetically by name for easier searching.

2. Prioritizing Tasks or Data

Sorting allows you to identify the most critical items quickly.

Example: Sort a to-do list by due date to prioritize urgent tasks.

3. Analyzing Performance Metrics

Sorting helps you focus on top-performing or underperforming areas.

Example: Sort sales data from highest to lowest to identify best-selling products.

4. Grouping Similar Data Together

You can group related information by sorting it by category.

Example: Organize employees by department to analyze team performance.

5. Finding Trends

Sorting data chronologically reveals patterns over time.

Example: Sort monthly revenue figures by date to track business growth.

6. Data Cleaning and Validation

Sorting helps you quickly identify duplicates, missing entries, or errors.

Example: Sort a list of email addresses to spot typos or duplicates.

7. Streamlining Reports

Sorting makes reports more presentable and easier to interpret.

Example: Sort survey responses by demographic to understand trends among different groups.

8. Customizing Presentations for Stakeholders

Tailor data for different audiences by sorting it to highlight specific insights.

Example: Sort budget figures by department when presenting to management.

9. Simplifying Comparisons

Sorting data allows for side-by-side comparisons of similar values.

Example: Sort exam scores from highest to lowest to see top performers.

10. Improving Decision-Making

Organized data provides clarity, making it easier to draw conclusions and make decisions.

Example: Sort expense reports by category to determine where to cut costs.

Filtering Data in Excel

Filtering lets you focus on specific data by hiding the rows that don't match your criteria. Here's how:

Select the Data Range.

- Highlight the area of your data, including the headers.
- Enable the Filter Option. Navigate to the **Data** tab on the ribbon.
- Click on **Filter**. Small drop-down arrows will appear in the header cells of your data.

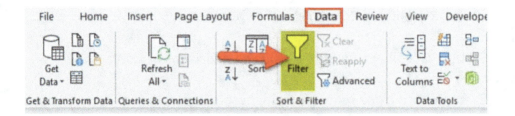

Filter by a Specific Value.

- Click the drop-down arrow in the column header you want to filter.

- Uncheck **Select All** to clear the current selections.

- Check the box next to the value(s) you want to display. For instance, to view only "Huawei" phones, check "Huawei."

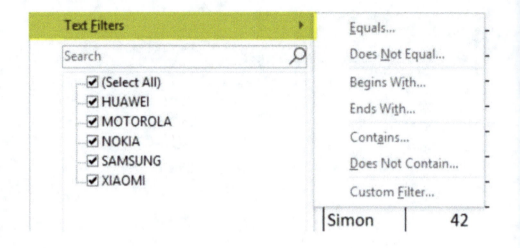

Filter by a Condition (Optional)

- For numbers, use conditions like "Greater Than," "Less Than," or "Between."
- For dates, filter by a specific range, such as "Last Month" or "Next Week."
- For text, filter by options like "Begins With" or "Contains." as in the last image.

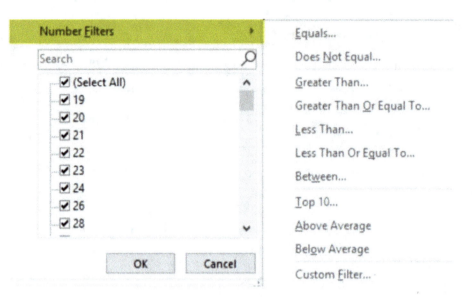

Data filter based on numbers

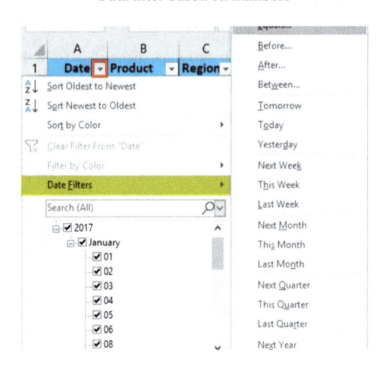

Data filter based on date values.

Apply and View Results

Once you select your filter criteria, Excel will hide the rows that don't meet the conditions. Only the relevant rows will remain visible.

Clear or Remove Filters

To remove a specific filter, click the drop-down arrow and choose **Clear Filter from [Column Name]**.

To remove all filters, go back to the **Data** tab and click **Clear** under the filter icon.

Practical application of filtering data in Excel

Filtering data in Microsoft Excel has various practical applications, especially when dealing with large datasets. Here are some common ways it can be used:

Finding Specific Information Quickly

- **Example**: In a sales report, you can filter to see only the transactions made by a specific salesperson or within a particular region.
- **Benefit**: Saves time by narrowing down thousands of rows to only what's relevant.

Analyzing Trends or Patterns

- **Example**: Filter by a date range to examine trends, such as sales during a holiday season or attendance in a specific month.
- **Benefit**: Helps in identifying patterns over time.

Focusing on Outliers or Exceptions

- **Example**: Filter to show only values greater than a certain threshold, like orders above $500 or expenses exceeding the budget.
- **Benefit**: Makes it easier to spot irregularities that need attention.

Comparing Categories or Groups

- **Example**: In a product inventory, filter by category to compare the stock levels of different product types.
- **Benefit**: Simplifies analysis by letting you focus on one group at a time.

Data Cleanup and Validation

- **Example**: Filter to find blank cells or duplicate entries in a dataset.
- **Benefit**: Makes it easier to spot and fix errors before using the data for analysis.

Creating Reports for Specific Audiences

- **Example**: Filter a performance report to show only the metrics relevant to a particular team or department.
- **Benefit**: Customizes data for better communication and decision-making.

Improving Efficiency in Decision-Making

- **Example**: Filter a supplier list to show only those located in a specific city to decide who to contact.
- **Benefit**: Enables informed and efficient decision-making.

Preparing for Further Analysis

- **Example**: Use filters to isolate data for export into another tool like a chart or pivot table.
- **Benefit**: Ensures that only the required subset of data is analyzed further.

Simplifying Visual Presentation

- **Example**: Filter to show only the top 10 values in a dataset, such as the best-performing products or employees.
- **Benefit**: Makes reports more concise and visually appealing.

Personalized Insights in Shared Files

- **Example**: Each team member can use filters to view only their relevant data in a shared project tracker.
- **Benefit**: Allows collaborative work without altering the original dataset for everyone.

Creating Simple Charts and Graphs

Before creating a chart or graph, you need data that Excel can represent visually. To visualize your data, you can create charts and graphs:

- Prepare Your Data. Open your Excel workbook and enter your data into a worksheet. Ensure your data is organized into rows and columns, with headers describing what each row or column represents (e.g., "Month" and "Sales").

	A	B	C	D	E	F
1		Jun	Jul	Aug	Sep	Oct
2	Oranges	100	120	130	105	90
3	Apples	210	230	225	190	185
4	Lemons	150	140	180	150	135

- Select the Data Range. Highlight the data you want to include in your chart. For example, if your data is in columns A and B from rows 1 to 6, click and drag to select A1:B6. Include the headers in your selection for clear labeling.

- Open the Chart Menu. Click the **Insert** tab. Click on the icon that best matches the type of chart you want to create. For example, if you want to show trends over time, choose a **Line Chart**. To compare different values, consider a **Bar Chart** or **Column Chart**. Hover over each chart type to see a preview of how your data will look in that format.

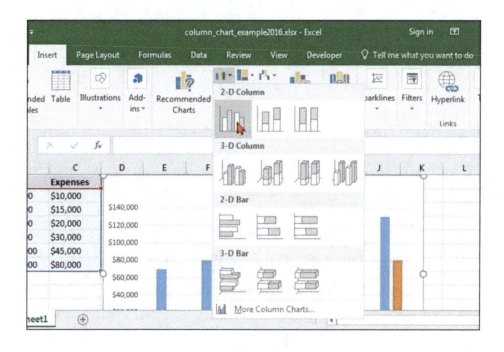

- Choose a Chart Type. Click on the icon that best matches the type of chart you want to create. For example, if you want to show trends over time, choose a **Line Chart**. To compare different values, consider a **Bar Chart** or **Column Chart**. Hover over each chart type to see a preview of how your data will look in that format.

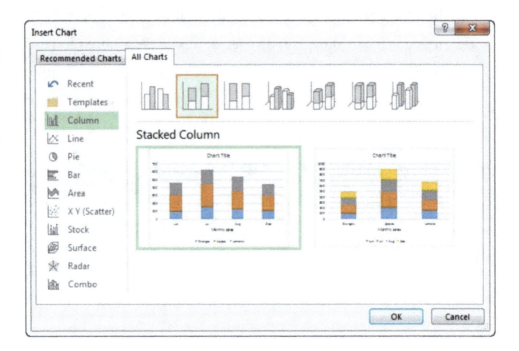

- Insert the Chart. After selecting a chart type, Excel will automatically create and display the chart on the worksheet. You can move the chart by clicking and dragging it to your desired location.

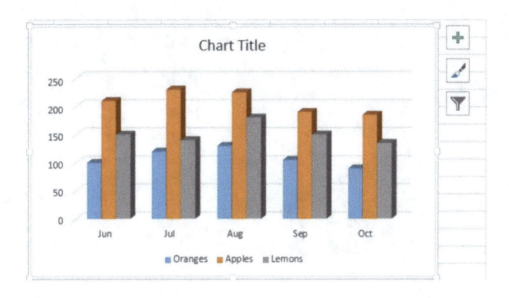

- Customize the Chart. Excel allows you to adjust the chart to better suit your needs. Add a chart title by clicking on the default title text box above the chart. Type in a descriptive title, such as "Monthly Sales."
- Adjust Axis Labels. Check if the axes (horizontal and vertical) are labeled correctly. You can modify them by right-clicking the axis and selecting **Format Axis**.

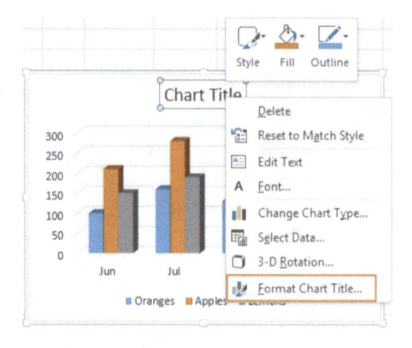

- Change Colors or Styles. Click on the chart and go to the **Chart Design** tab. Choose from different styles or colors to make your chart visually appealing.

- Resize and Position the Chart. Click and drag the edges of the chart to resize it. Position the chart within the worksheet for better visibility.

- Save your Excel file to ensure you don't lose your chart. Click **File**, then **Save As**, and choose a location to store your file.

Practical Applications of Using Charts and Graphs

Charts and graphs in Excel have numerous practical applications across various fields. They help in simplifying data, identifying patterns, and supporting decision-making. Here are some key applications:

1. Business and Financial Analysis

- **Sales Tracking:** Visualize monthly, quarterly, or yearly sales trends to monitor growth.
- **Expense Management:** Analyze spending patterns through pie charts or bar graphs to identify cost-saving opportunities.
- **Profit Margins:** Compare revenue and expenses over time to evaluate profitability.
- **Market Trends:** Represent market shares or customer preferences for informed strategic planning.

2. Project Management

- **Progress Monitoring:** Use Gantt charts or progress graphs to track project timelines and milestones.
- **Resource Allocation:** Visualize how resources like time, budget, or personnel are distributed across tasks.
- **Risk Analysis:** Represent potential risks and their impact using bubble charts or scatter plots.

3. Education and Training

- **Performance Tracking:** Show students' grades over time with line or column charts.
- **Comparative Analysis:** Compare results across different groups or timeframes to identify learning trends.
- **Survey Results:** Represent feedback from surveys or evaluations to improve educational methods.

4. Personal Use

- **Budget Planning:** Visualize household income and expenses to create a manageable budget.
- **Fitness Tracking:** Track weight loss, exercise routines, or diet plans over time.
- **Investment Growth:** Use charts to monitor the performance of personal investments or savings.

5. Research and Data Analysis

- **Statistical Studies:** Represent experimental data to identify correlations or trends.
- **Data Summarization:** Summarize large datasets into digestible visual formats for presentations.
- **Predictive Analysis:** Use trendlines in graphs to forecast future data points.

6. Marketing and Advertising

- **Audience Insights:** Represent demographic data or customer preferences for targeted campaigns.
- **Campaign Performance:** Track key metrics like engagement, reach, or conversions through line or bar charts.
- **Competitor Analysis:** Compare your performance against competitors to identify opportunities for improvement.

7. Human Resources

- **Employee Performance:** Use charts to evaluate employee performance or productivity.
- **Recruitment Statistics:** Represent hiring trends or attrition rates to refine recruitment strategies.
- **Training Effectiveness:** Monitor the impact of training programs over time.

8. Healthcare and Medicine

- **Patient Monitoring:** Visualize health data like blood pressure or glucose levels over time.
- **Epidemiology:** Analyze the spread of diseases using data visualization tools.
- **Resource Planning:** Represent hospital occupancy rates or staff allocation visually.

9. Supply Chain and Logistics

- **Inventory Management:** Use charts to track stock levels and avoid overstocking or understocking.
- **Delivery Timelines:** Represent delivery times to monitor logistics performance.
- **Cost Analysis:** Visualize shipping costs across different routes or methods.

10. Government and Policy Making

- **Census Data Analysis:** Visualize population data for policy planning.
- **Budget Allocation:** Represent government spending across sectors.
- **Public Awareness:** Use charts to present data in a way that is accessible to the public.

Why Charts and Graphs Are Essential:

- They simplify complex data into an easy-to-understand visual format.
- They make trends and relationships in data more apparent.
- They enhance presentations, making them more engaging and professional.

- They support better decision-making by providing a clear overview of the data.

Working with Multiple Sheets and Workbooks

When working with Excel, you often need to manage multiple sheets and workbooks for complex tasks. Here's a step-by-step guide on effectively handling these features:

1. Navigating Between Sheets

- **View Sheet Tabs**: At the bottom of your Excel workbook, you'll see tabs labeled "Sheet1," "Sheet2," etc.
- **Switch Between Sheets**: Click on any tab to view its content.
- **Use Keyboard Shortcuts**: Press Ctrl + PgUp or Ctrl + PgDn to move between sheets quickly.

2. Adding, Renaming, and Deleting Sheets

- **Add a New Sheet**: Click the "+" icon next to the existing sheet tabs.

1. Locate and select the **New sheet** button near the bottom-right corner of the Excel window.

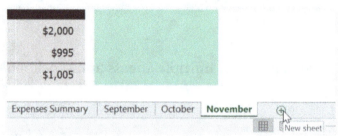

2. A **new blank worksheet** will appear.

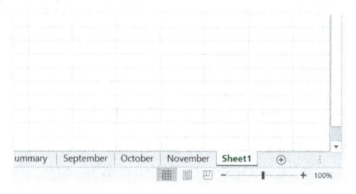

- **Rename a Sheet**: Right-click the sheet tab you want to rename. Select **Rename**, then type a new name.

Right-click the **worksheet** you want to rename, then select **Rename** from the worksheet menu.

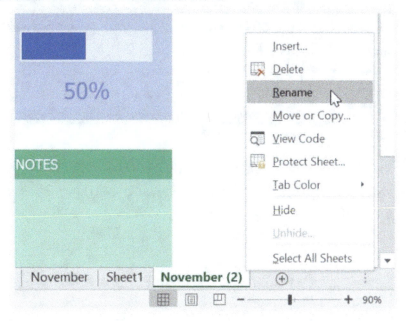

- **Delete a Sheet**: Right-click the sheet tab. Choose **Delete** (Ensure no critical data is on that sheet before deleting).

3. Grouping Sheets for Simultaneous Editing

- **Select Multiple Sheets**: Hold down Ctrl and click each sheet tab you want to group. Alternatively, hold Shift to select a range of consecutive sheets.

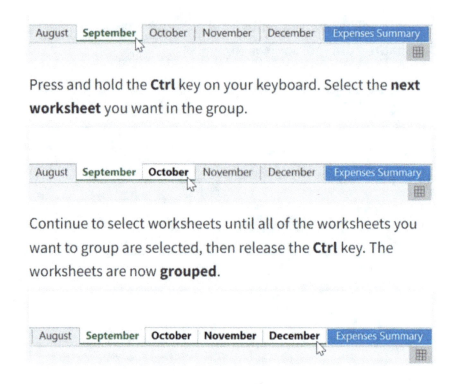

Press and hold the **Ctrl** key on your keyboard. Select the **next worksheet** you want in the group.

Continue to select worksheets until all of the worksheets you want to group are selected, then release the **Ctrl** key. The worksheets are now **grouped**.

- **Make Changes**: Any changes you make (like formatting or data entry) will apply to all grouped sheets.
- **Ungroup Sheets**: Right-click on a sheet tab and select **Ungroup Sheets**.

Right-click a worksheet in the group, then select **Ungroup Sheets** from the worksheet menu.

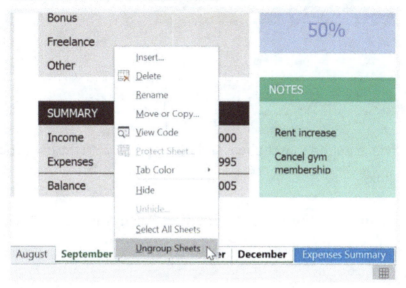

4. Linking Data Between Sheets

Linking data between sheets ensures that updates in one sheet reflect automatically in another.

- **Start with the Destination Cell**: Go to the cell where you want the linked data to appear.
- **Enter the Formula**: Type = to start a formula.

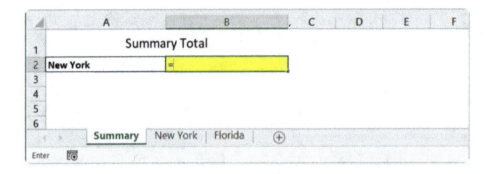

Navigate to the source sheet and click the cell with the data you want to link.

- **Complete the Link**: Press Enter. The destination cell will now display the value from the source cell.

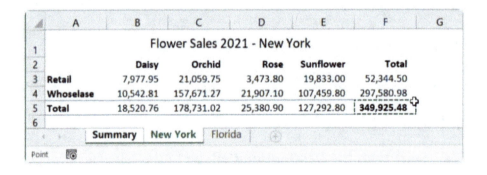

- **Understand the Formula**: For example, if you're linking data from cell A1 in Sheet1 to Sheet2, the formula in Sheet2 might look like this: =Sheet1!A1. In the example image above and below, the formula is ='New York'!F5

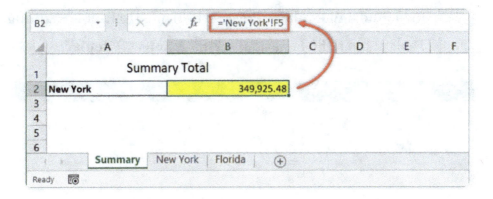

5. Linking Data Between Workbooks

If your data is in different workbooks, the process is similar:

- **Open Both Workbooks**: Ensure both are open in Excel.
- **Enter the Formula**: In the destination workbook, type =. Switch to the source workbook, click the desired cell, and press Enter.
- **Save Both Workbooks**: Remember, the link will break if you move or delete the source workbook without updating the link.

6. Using Find and Replace Across Sheets

Excel's Find and Replace feature can save time when editing data across multiple sheets. The purpose of the **Find and Replace Across Sheets** feature in Excel is to streamline the process of locating and updating data across multiple sheets in a workbook. This feature is particularly useful in scenarios where you need to make consistent edits or corrections to data that is spread across different sheets.

- **Open Find and Replace**: Press Ctrl + H or go to **Home > Editing** (Tools at top right hand side**) > Find & Select > Replace**.

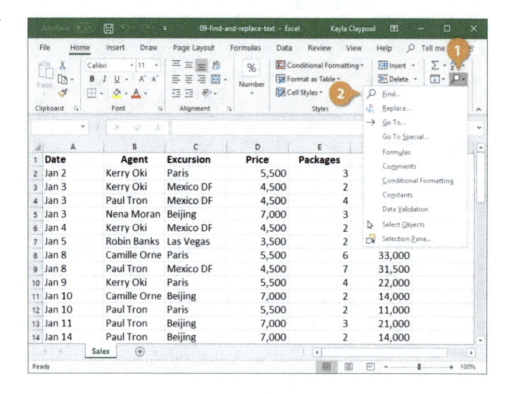

- **Set Your Search Scope**: Click **Options** in the Find and Replace window. Under **Within**, select **Workbook** to search across all sheets. **Enter Your Search Terms**: In the **Find What** box, type the data you're looking for.

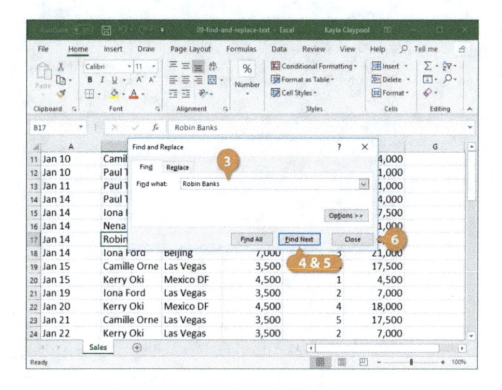

Follow the images guide above (1-6). Click **Find Next** to move to other occurrences of the word. Use **Find All** to find the cell location of all similar instances at once. Select **Close** when you're finished. Repeat guide (1-2). This time select **Replace**.

In the **Replace with** box, type the new data.

Execute the Replacement:

Click **Replace All** to update all matches at once or **Find Next** to replace them one at a time.

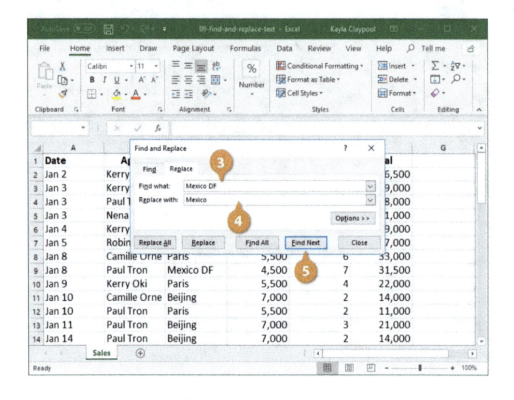

Saving and Sharing Excel Files

Cloud Syncing with OneDrive

To save your Excel files to OneDrive and ensure cloud syncing:

- Click **File** > **Save As** > **OneDrive**. This ensures your file is automatically backed up and accessible from any device.

We will discuss saving with OneDrive more extensively in a subsequent chapter.

Exporting Excel Files to PDF

To export an Excel file as a PDF:

- Click **File** > **Export** > **Create PDF/XPS**. Choose where to save the PDF and select **Publish**.

This feature is helpful when you need to share your workbook as a read-only file.

Keyboard Shortcuts

Microsoft Word Keyboard Shortcuts

Basic File Operations

1. **Create a New Document**: Ctrl + N

   Opens a new blank document.

2. **Open an Existing Document**: Ctrl + O

   Opens the file browser to locate and open a saved document.

3. **Save the Document**: Ctrl + S

   Saves the current document.

4. **Save As**: F12

   Opens the "Save As" dialog box.

5. **Print**: Ctrl + P

   Opens the print dialog box.

Editing Text

1. **Undo the Last Action**: Ctrl + Z

   Reverts the most recent change.

2. **Redo the Last Undo**: Ctrl + Y

   Re-applies the last undone action.

3. **Cut Text**: Ctrl + X

   Removes the selected text and copies it to the clipboard.

4. **Copy Text**: Ctrl + C

   Copies the selected text to the clipboard.

5. **Paste Text**: Ctrl + V

   Inserts the content from the clipboard at the cursor.

Navigation

1. **Move to the Start of the Document**: Ctrl + Home
2. **Move to the End of the Document**: Ctrl + End
3. **Select Text**:
   - Select All: Ctrl + A
   - Select to the Beginning of the Line: Shift + Home
   - Select to the End of the Line: Shift + End
4. **Search**: Ctrl + F

   Opens the navigation pane to search for text.

Formatting

1. **Bold Text**: Ctrl + B
2. **Italicize Text**: Ctrl + I
3. **Underline Text**: Ctrl + U
4. **Align Text**:
   - Left Align: Ctrl + L

- Center Align: Ctrl + E
- Right Align: Ctrl + R
- Justify: Ctrl + J

5. **Apply Heading Style**:

Alt + Shift + 1 (Heading 1), Alt + Shift + 2 (Heading 2), etc.

Microsoft Excel Keyboard Shortcuts

Basic File Operations

1. **Create a New Workbook**: Ctrl + N
2. **Open a Workbook**: Ctrl + O
3. **Save the Workbook**: Ctrl + S
4. **Close Workbook**: Ctrl + W

Navigation

1. **Move to the Next Cell**: Tab
2. **Move to the Previous Cell**: Shift + Tab
3. **Go to the First Cell in the Worksheet**: Ctrl + Home
4. **Go to the Last Cell with Data**: Ctrl + End
5. **Open the Go To Dialog Box**: Ctrl + G or F5

Editing

1. **Edit the Active Cell**: F2
2. **Cut Cell Content**: Ctrl + X
3. **Copy Cell Content**: Ctrl + C
4. **Paste Cell Content**: Ctrl + V
5. **Insert a New Line within a Cell**: Alt + Enter
6. **Delete Cell Content**: Delete

Selecting Cells

1. **Select the Entire Worksheet**: Ctrl + A
2. **Select the Entire Row**: Shift + Space
3. **Select the Entire Column**: Ctrl + Space
4. **Extend Selection to the Last Cell in the Row/Column**: Shift + Ctrl + Arrow Key

Formulas and Calculations

1. **Insert a Formula**: Alt + =
   Automatically sums the selected cells.
2. **Recalculate Formulas**: F9
3. **Display All Formulas**: Ctrl + ~
4. **Open the Insert Function Dialog Box**: Shift + F3

Formatting

1. **Bold Text**: Ctrl + B
2. **Italicize Text**: Ctrl + I
3. **Add Borders**: Ctrl + Shift + &
4. **Apply Number Format**: Ctrl + Shift + 1
5. **Apply Currency Format**: Ctrl + Shift + $
6. **Apply Percentage Format**: Ctrl + Shift + %

Working with Worksheets

1. **Add a New Worksheet**: Shift + F11
2. **Switch Between Worksheets**:

   Ctrl + Page Up (previous), Ctrl + Page Down (next)
3. **Rename a Worksheet**: Alt + H + O + R
4. **Delete a Worksheet**: Alt + H + D + S

Appendices

Appendix A: Microsoft Office 365 Tools Comparison: Word Vs Excel

This appendix provides a detailed comparison of all the key tools discussed throughout the guide. By understanding the strengths and unique features of each tool, you will be better equipped to choose the right one for your specific needs. This table will help you understand the core functionalities and how each tool fits into the broader Office 365 suite. It also highlights key differences between similar tools, so you can make informed decisions when deciding which tool to use.

125

Tool	Primary Function	Key Features	When to Use	Key Differences
Microsoft Word	Document creation and editing	Text formatting, templates, styles, collaboration, integration with OneDrive	Use when creating text-heavy documents, to reports, and letters.	More document-focused compared to Excel and other Microsoft suites.
Microsoft Excel	Data organization, analysis, and calculation	Pivot tables, data charts, formulas, data validation, cell formatting, filtering.	Use for handling numbers, data analysis, and financial models.	Best for numerical analysis; not ideal for text-heavy documents.

Appendix B: Troubleshooting Common Issues

This section offers solutions to common issues you may encounter while using Microsoft Office 365 tools. These troubleshooting steps will help you resolve issues quickly and get back to your tasks without unnecessary delays.

Troubleshooting Common Issues in Microsoft Word

1. **Problem**: Word is Running Slowly or Freezing

Cause: Too many open files, large documents, or insufficient computer memory.

Solution:

- Close unnecessary Word documents or programs running in the background.
- Save your document, close Word, and restart your computer.
- Open Word again and check if the problem persists.
- If it still runs slowly, disable unnecessary add-ins:
- Open Word, click on **File** > **Options** > **Add-ins**.
- Choose "COM Add-ins" from the dropdown at the bottom, and click **Go**.
- Uncheck any add-ins you don't need and restart Word.

128

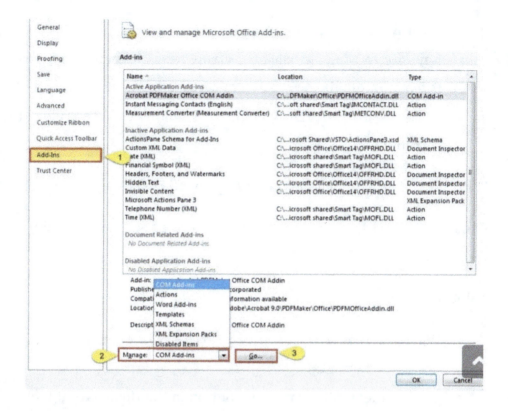

2. **Problem**: Word File Won't Open

Cause: The file might be corrupted or created in an incompatible version of Word.

Solution:

- Ensure the file is saved in a Word-compatible format (.docx or .doc).
- Right-click the file and select **Open with > Microsoft Word**.
- If the file doesn't open, use the Word Repair tool:

- Open Word and click **File** > **Open**.

- Navigate to your file, click the arrow next to **Open**, and select **Open and Repair**.

- If this doesn't work, try opening it on another device to rule out corruption.

3. **Problem**: Formatting Issues (Text Alignment, Fonts, etc.)

Cause: Copy-pasting from other sources often brings hidden formatting.

Solution:

- Highlight the text and press **Ctrl + Spacebar** to remove unwanted formatting.

- Use the **Clear All Formatting** button in the Home tab (it looks like an eraser with an A).

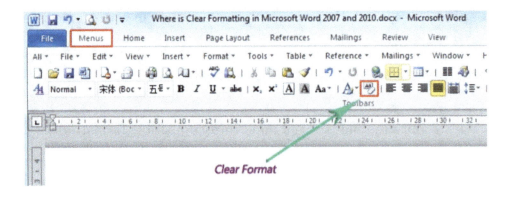

Clear Format

- Copy text into Notepad first to strip formatting, then paste it back into Word.

4. **Problem**: Can't Find a Recently Saved File

Cause: File may have been saved in a different location or under an unfamiliar name.

Solution:

- Open Word and go to **File > Recent** to check recent documents.
- Use your computer's search feature to look for the file:
- Type part of the file name or ".docx" into the search bar.
- Save documents regularly using **Ctrl + S** to avoid future issues.

5. **Problem**: Spelling and Grammar Checker Not Working

Cause: Language settings might be incorrect, or the feature is turned off.

Solution:

- Go to **File > Options > Proofing**.
- Make sure **Check spelling as you type** and **Mark grammar errors as you type** are checked.

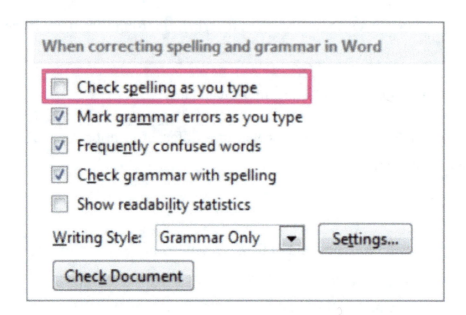

- Ensure the correct language is set:

- Highlight the text, go to **Review** > **Language** > **Set Proofing Language**, and select your preferred language.

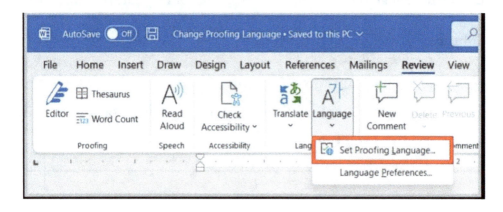

6. **Problem**: Word is Not Responding

Cause: Conflicts with other programs or issues with the Word installation.

Solution:

- Wait for a minute; sometimes, Word needs time to process large files.
- Press **Ctrl + Alt + Delete** and open Task Manager. Find Microsoft Word, click on it, and select **End Task**.
- Restart Word. If it crashes again, start Word in Safe Mode:
- Hold **Ctrl** while opening Word and click **Yes** when prompted.
- If the problem continues, repair Word:
- Go to **Control Panel** > **Programs and Features**.
- Find Microsoft Office, right-click it, and select **Change** > **Repair**.

7. **Problem**: Images or Text Disappear When Printing

Cause: Printer settings or outdated printer drivers.

Solution:

- Ensure you're using the correct printer:
- Go to **File** > **Print** and check the printer name.
- Update your printer driver by visiting the printer manufacturer's website.

- Check if the issue is with the document:
- Try printing another document to see if the problem persists.
- If only certain elements disappear, save the file as a PDF and print the PDF instead.

8. **Problem**: Table of Contents Won't Update

Cause: Manual edits to the Table of Contents or incorrect heading styles.

Solution:

- Ensure headings are formatted correctly using styles like **Heading 1**, **Heading 2**, etc.
- Click on the Table of Contents, then select **Update Table** and choose to update the entire table.

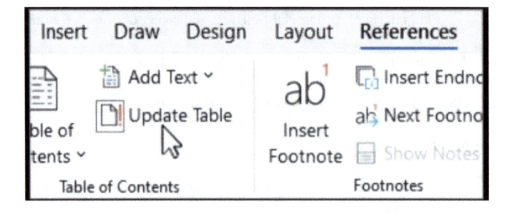

- Avoid manually typing in the Table of Contents; use Word's automated tool instead.

9. **Problem**: Word Keeps Crashing

Cause: Corrupted templates or add-ins.

Solution:

- Rename the Normal.dotm template:
- Navigate   to **C:\Users[YourUserName]\AppData\Roaming\Microsoft\Templates**.
- Rename **Normal.dotm** to **Normal_old.dotm** and restart Word.
- Disable add-ins:
- Open Word in Safe Mode (hold **Ctrl** while starting Word).
- Disable unnecessary add-ins through **File** > **Options** > **Add-ins**.

Troubleshooting Common Issues in Microsoft Excel

1. Excel is Slow or Freezing

Sometimes Excel may become slow or unresponsive, especially when working with large files or multiple functions.

Steps to Fix:

Step 1: **Close Unnecessary Programs**

Having too many programs open can slow down your computer. Close unused apps to free up memory.

Step 2: **Disable Add-ins**

Go to **File** > **Options** > **Add-ins**. Under **Manage**, choose **COM Add-ins** and click **Go**. Uncheck any add-ins you don't use and click **OK**.

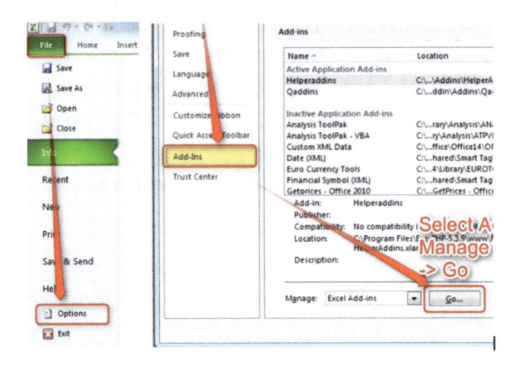

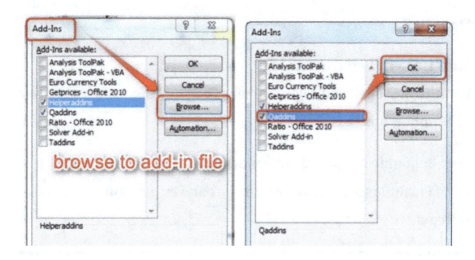

browse to add-in file

Step 3: **Optimize File Size**

If your file is large, try deleting unnecessary data, unused sheets, or conditional formatting that may be slowing things down.

Step 4: **Update Excel**

Go to **File > Account > Update Options** and ensure Excel is updated to the latest version.

2. Formulas Are Not Calculating

When formulas show as plain text instead of calculating results, it can be frustrating.

Steps to Fix:

Step 1: **Check Cell Formatting**

Right-click the cell and select **Format Cells**. Ensure it is set to **General** or **Number**, not **Text**.

Step 2: **Enable Automatic Calculations**

Go to **Formulas** > **Calculation Options** and ensure **Automatic** is selected.

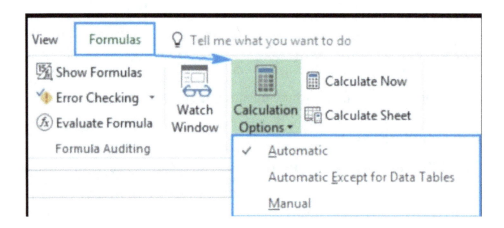

Step 3: **Look for Errors in the Formula**

Verify the formula syntax. For example, ensure every parenthesis is correctly paired.

3. Cells Display #####

This happens when the content in a cell is too wide for the column.

Steps to Fix:

Step 1: Adjust Column Width

Hover over the edge of the column header, then drag it to make the column wider. Alternatively, double-click the column edge for auto-fit.

Step 2: Reduce Content Size

If adjusting the column is not an option, reduce the font size or wrap the text by clicking **Wrap Text** in the **Home** tab.

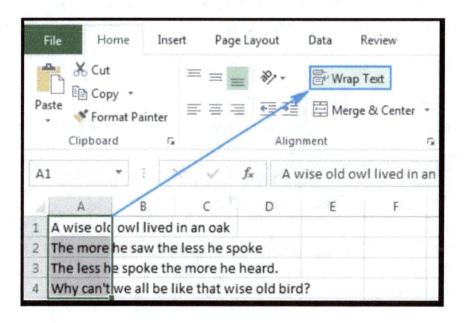

4. Cannot Open an Excel File

If an Excel file refuses to open, the file might be corrupted or incompatible.

Steps to Fix:

Step 1: Repair the File

Open Excel, go to **File > Open**, and locate your file. Click the dropdown arrow next to **Open** and select **Open and Repair**.

Step 2: Check Compatibility

If the file was created in a different version of Excel, save it in a compatible format. Go to **File > Save As**, and choose **Excel Workbook (.xlsx)**.

Step 3: Copy Data to a New File

If the file opens but behaves strangely, copy the data into a new workbook.

5. Error Messages (e.g., #DIV/0!, #REF!)

These errors often appear due to formula mistakes or missing data.

Steps to Fix:

Step 1: Understand the Error Type

Hover over the error to see an explanation. For example, **#DIV/0!** means you're dividing by zero.

Step 2: Correct the Issue

For **#DIV/0!**, ensure you are not dividing by a blank cell or zero. Use the formula =IF(B2=0, "", A2/B2) to avoid the error.

For **#REF!**, check if a cell used in the formula has been deleted.

Step 3: Use the Error Checker

Go to **Formulas** > **Error Checking** to identify and resolve errors automatically.

6. Excel Crashes During Printing

Printing issues can be due to incorrect printer settings or corrupted drivers.

Steps to Fix:

Step 1: Check Printer Settings

Go to **File** > **Print** and verify the correct printer is selected.

Step 2: Update or Reinstall Printer Drivers

Visit your printer manufacturer's website to update or reinstall the drivers.

Step 3: **Simplify Your Spreadsheet**

Remove unnecessary graphics or images, as they can cause Excel to crash when printing.

7. Can't Edit a Shared Workbook

When using shared workbooks, editing may sometimes be restricted.

Steps to Fix:

Step 1: **Check Permissions**

Ensure you have the proper permissions to edit the file. Contact the owner if needed.

Step 2: **Unprotect the Workbook**

Go to **Review > Unprotect Workbook** and enter the password if required.

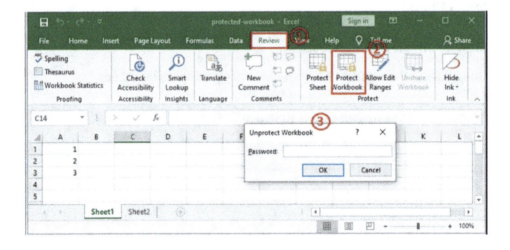

Step 3: Enable Editing

If the workbook is in read-only mode, click **Enable Editing** at the top of the window.

8. Copy-Paste Isn't Working

This issue might arise due to settings or clipboard errors.

Steps to Fix:

Step 1: Clear the Clipboard

Press **Ctrl + Shift + Esc** to open the Task Manager, then close any clipboard-related processes.

Step 2: Check Paste Options

Right-click and review the paste options. Use **Paste Values** if formulas are causing issues.

Step 3: Restart Excel

Save your work, close Excel, and reopen it to refresh the clipboard functionality.

9. Workbook Opens Blank

If a workbook opens but shows a blank screen, it could be due to display settings.

Steps to Fix:

Step 1: **Unhide Worksheets**

Go to **View** > **Unhide** and select the hidden sheet.

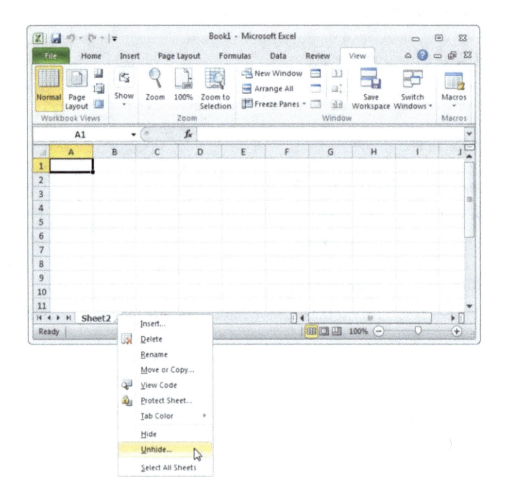

Step 2: **Check for Hidden Columns or Rows**

Select the entire worksheet, right-click, and choose **Unhide**.

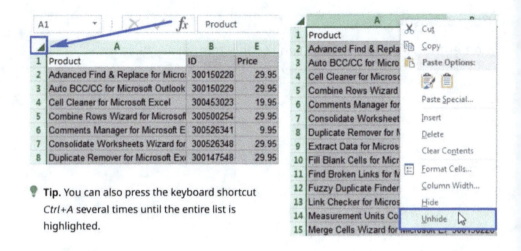

Tip. You can also press the keyboard shortcut *Ctrl+A* several times until the entire list is highlighted.

Step 3: Adjust Window Settings

Go to **View** > **Arrange All** and choose **Cascade** to bring the workbook into view.

10. Keyboard Shortcuts Aren't Working

If shortcuts like **Ctrl + C** or **Ctrl + Z** don't work, there might be a conflict.

Steps to Fix:

Step 1: Check Your Keyboard

Ensure the **Ctrl** key isn't stuck or damaged.

Step 2: Restore Default Shortcuts

Go to **File** > **Options** > **Customize Ribbon**, and reset the keyboard shortcuts to default.

Step 3: Restart Excel

Sometimes, a simple restart can resolve temporary glitches.

Appendix C: Glossary of Key Terms

This glossary provides definitions of the key terms used throughout this guide. Understanding these terms will help reinforce your learning and ensure that you are comfortable with the terminology associated with Microsoft Office 365.

- **Add-ins**: Optional features or tools that extend the functionality of Office applications. For example, in Word, you can install add-ins that help with referencing or document design.

- **Conditional Formatting**: A feature in Excel and other applications that allows you to format cells based on specific criteria, such as highlighting values greater than a certain number.

- **Pivot Tables**: A data summarization tool in Excel that is used to automatically sort, count, and total the data stored in a database.

- **Version History**: A feature in **Word** that allows you to track and restore previous versions of a document or file.

- **Workspace**: The area in Office applications like Word and Excel where you work on your files. It is also where the document, spreadsheet, or presentation is displayed for editing.

Index

www.ingramcontent.com/pod-product-compliance
Lightning Source LLC
LaVergne TN
LVHW051735050326
832903LV00023B/928